# The Masters P

CW00809279

## Checklists

Captain Michael Lloyd, FNI

Senior Advisor, Witherby Seamanship International Ltd

First edition published 2009

ISBN 978 1 905331 44 4

© Witherby Seamanship International Ltd, 2009

**British Library Cataloguing in Publication Data**
A catalogue record for this book is available from the British Library.

Printed and bound in Great Britain by Bell & Bain Ltd, Glasgow

Published in 2009 by

**Witherby Seamanship International Ltd**
4 Dunlop Square, Livingston
Edinburgh, EH54 8SB
Scotland, UK

Tel No:  +44(0)1506 463 227
Fax No: +44(0)1506 468 999

Email: info@emailws.com
www.witherbyseamanship.com

# Author's Introduction

A ship, because of the environment in which it operates, has to be well ordered. This means that set routines have to be established for the various functions and procedures to ensure maximum efficiency and the safety of all onboard. With the general system of relieving, most commercial ships exist in a state of constant change of the officers responsible for its management. An established routine of order and responsibility ensures a smooth transition and a continuation of the management while the new officer settles into the ship and his position. Changes can then be made within the established procedure and with the acceptance of all others who may be affected by them.

Under the International Safety Management (ISM) Code, a vessel must operate within the framework and requirements of the Safety Management System (SMS). It is not intended to replace any system but to provide further support, reference and thought for those who wish to improve their systems onboard.

Another reason is it avoids conflict in areas where responsibilities overlap, or where there are 'dead' zones, with each officer thinking that the other is dealing with a certain problem when, in actual fact, no one is taking responsibility.

While not intended to conflict with laid down company procedures, which are often written as general regulations for all ships in their fleet, such a local management system enables adaptation to the circumstances onboard that particular ship, at that time.

Finally, it allows the command to change without disruption and provides the new Master a picture of how the ship management is presently functioning. This makes it easier for him to work within that organisation and to change whatever parts of the management he wishes should he choose to do so.

This book contains shipboard management procedures for all of the main management functions. These procedures are written and allocated to responsible officers purely as an indication of how responsibility can be allotted. They can be adapted to whatever circumstances and personnel exist onboard.

Ship and engine maintenance have been excluded as they fall within the province of these departments and each department should have its own management functions.

It is impossible to cover all functions or to have a procedure for all eventualities, especially in such a complicated environment as a ship, but by using these procedures and common sense, the ship and those on it will benefit from an organised system.

Why am I using checklists? Well, 'senior moments' do not only occur with seniors, they happen to us all regardless of age. That cold feeling you get when going to your cabin after clearing the port and you suddenly realise that the agent did not return the ship's trading documents, or when you go to the cabin and see all the crew and official mail still waiting for posting and the ship is off for a forty day haul will make you realise the usefulness of lists.

Finally, I must offer thanks to Ronald Wöhrn, a Master Mariner and a Lawyer at Ahlers & Vogel, who authored the 'Guidance to Masters' manual and kindly allowed access to his publication for the benefit of this title on 'Masters Checklists'.

Captain Michael Lloyd, FNI

# CONTENTS

# 1 Safety Items

Safety items are always at the top of the list when surveys and inspections are carried out. The ship, while realising the importance of these items, will have other work to get on with as well, so it is important that, as Master, you lay down robust procedures to cover the care of safety items. In addition to the obvious dangers, too often it is the failure to take such care that causes delay to your vessel through the need to make corrections before the ship can sail.

A proper procedure should cover exactly which department is responsible for what, the Safety Officer's responsibility and the documentation and maintenance of all equipment.

## 1.1 Departmental Responsibilities

- The Shipboard Safety Officer's responsibilities are as designated in the Safety Management System
- the Electrical Officer tests should be reported to the Engine Department management team and deficiencies to the Safety Officer
- the Radio Officer should report deficiencies to the Safety Officer.

## 1.2   Safety Equipment on Deck

Action Officer: 3rd Officer/Deck Officer of the 8 to 12 watch

### 1.2.1   Maintenance

- All deck equipment must be maintained using a planned maintenance system
- a log book must be kept and all maintenance must be recorded. This log should be signed weekly by the Chief Officer and monthly by the Master
- the Chief Officer should arrange to have available any crew that are required by the Safety Officer for maintenance purposes.

### 1.2.2   Defects

If shipboard repairs are required:

- ☑ The Chief Officer must be notified
- ☑ a repair request should be made to the head of the department that is required to make the repair
- ☑ once it is completed, the repair must be logged in the departmental Safety Log Book
- ☑ the Chief Officer must advise the management team of all safety repairs in that week.

If shore repair or assistance is required:

- ☑ Shore repairs are decided by the Chief Officer
- ☑ the Chief Officer/Chief Engineer should make out the appropriate landing form
- ☑ if necessary, the company should be advised
- ☑ any shore technician should be accompanied by the Safety Officer and departmental Safety Representative
- ☑ the Safety Officer must advise the departmental head, Master and Safety Committee once the repair has been carried out to his satisfaction
- ☑ the completion of the repair must be logged in the Safety Log Book
- ☑ the Safety Officer must advise the company through the Master that the repair has been completed.

## 1.3    Safety Equipment in the Engine Room

Action Officer: 4th Engineer/Officer keeping the 8 to 12 watch and the designated Safety Officer

### 1.3.1   Maintenance

- All engine space equipment must be maintained under a planned maintenance system
- a log book must be kept and all safety maintenance work must be recorded. This should be signed weekly by the 2nd Engineer
- the 2nd Engineer must arrange to have available any crew that are required by the departmental Safety Officer for maintenance purposes.

### 1.3.2   Defects

If shipboard repairs are required:

- ☑ The Safety Officer must be notified
- ☑ a repair request must be issued to the head of the department that will make the repair
- ☑ the repair must be noted as a priority and treated as such
- ☑ the Safety Officer must be informed when the repair is completed
- ☑ the repair should be entered in the departmental Safety Log Book.

If shore repair or assistance is required:

- ☑ Any shore repair must be agreed by the Safety Officer
- ☑ the 2nd Engineer must make out the appropriate landing form
- ☑ the 2nd Engineer must advise the Master and the Chief Engineer
- ☑ the Safety Officer must advise the company
- ☑ the Safety Officer should accompany any shore technician attending
- ☑ the 2nd Engineer must confirm to the Safety Officer that the repair has been carried out to his satisfaction

- ☑ the 2nd Engineer should sign the work sheet stating that he is signing only for the work that has been done
- ☑ the repair should be logged in the departmental Safety Log
- ☑ the Safety Officer must notify the Master, Chief Engineer and the company that the repair has been completed.

## 1.4   Safety Stores/Safety Spares

Action Officer: Safety Officer

- The Safety Officer is responsible for the care and issue of all safety stores
- requisitions for new stores and spares must be made through the Chief Officer or Chief Engineer (as appropriate)
- the engine department should initially requisition stores from the Safety Officer. If these are not onboard, he must then requisition them through the Chief Officer or Chief Engineer (as appropriate)
- the Safety Officer must keep a list of safety stores and spares onboard.

## 1.5    Safety Surveys

A safety survey fulfils two objectives. The first is to ensure that all of the equipment is in good order. The second is an indirect inspection of the management of the safety aspects of the vessel. A poor finding reflects on you, which is a good enough reason to ensure that all is ready for the surveyor.

Action Officers: Chief Engineer, Chief Officer and Safety Officer

- ☑  The company's head office/the ship manager is responsible for arranging safety surveys
- ☑  after receiving notification, the Chief Officer should advise the Chief Engineer and Safety Officer of the survey
- ☑  the Safety Officer must check and prepare the equipment according to the safety survey checklist. Once everything is in order, the Safety Officer should be informed that the department is ready for inspection
- ☑  the Safety Officer should notify the Master when the ship is ready to be surveyed, or must give reasons why it is not
- ☑  the surveyor should always be accompanied on the survey by the appropriate Department Head and Safety Officer
- ☑  when the survey is completed, the Safety Officer should accompany the surveyor to the Master
- ☑  the Master and the Safety Officer should discuss the survey with the surveyor. Repair of any defects noted must be put in hand and, where necessary, equipment should be ordered
- ☑  the company should be notified of the results of the survey.

## 1.6    Shipboard Safety Meetings

Action Officer: Safety Officer and Departmental Safety Representatives

Further general information on meetings can be found in chapter 6.

- ☑ Safety meetings should be held monthly
- ☑ The Master will normally chair the meeting and introduce the agenda, which should include the following:
  - near misses and any accidents onboard
  - near misses and accidents in the fleet
  - important safety messages from the company
  - any outstanding safety non-conformities
  - any recent changes in the industry
- ☑ all Safety Committee members must attend the meeting
- ☑ a copy of the safety meeting minutes should be given to the Master, Chief Engineer and Chief Officer, placed in the Safety Meeting file in both the officer and crew recreation rooms and posted on notice boards.

## 1.7    Drills and Exercises

If you are to have a drill, it is better to have a meaningful one and, for example, the regular lowering of boats gets crew into a routine that becomes familiar and normal.

Action Officers: Chief Officer and Safety Officer

Where possible, you should use any available time in port or while awaiting orders to conduct drills so that the ship's business is not delayed. Each drill should be planned to ensure that, on a rotating basis, all safety equipment is used and training is given in its use.

■    Drills should be held each week to either meet or exceed the requirements of the Flag State and other guidelines
■    during these drills, the boats should be lowered, weather permitting, to the boat deck
■    normally, an exercise is held as part of the drill routine.

Exercises should cover the following drills:

| Statutory Drill Type | Intervals Not Exceeding |
|---|---|
| Abandon Ship | 1 month |
| Fire | 1 month |
| Enclosed Space Entry | 2 months |
| Lifeboat Launched and Manoeuvred in Water* | 3 months |
| Rescue Boat Drill | 3 months |
| Emergency Steering | 3 months |
| ISPS Security Drill | 3 months |
| Davit Launch Liferaft | 4 months |

If more than 25% of crew change, an abandon ship drill and a fire drill should be completed within 24 hours after leaving port. If it is not practical to hold full drills, musters should be held within the 24 hours with instruction given to the crew on their emergency duties and on abandon ship.

* Freefall lifeboats can be launched every 6 months if lowered every 3 months, or extended to 12 months if simulation requirements are met.

| Non-Statutory Drills | Suggested Interval |
|---|---|
| Personal Injury/First Aid | 6 weeks |
| Anti-Piracy | 6 weeks |
| Oil Spill/Pollution | 6 weeks |
| Main Engine Failure | 3 months |
| Toxic Vapour Release | 3 months |
| Power Failure | 3 months |
| Man Overboard | 6 months |
| Helicopter Evacuation | 6 months |
| Grounding/Stranding | 6 months |
| Collision | 6 months |
| Break Away from Berth | 6 months |
| Hull Damage/Flooding | 12 months |
| Emergency Towing | 12 months |
| First Alert Notification | Change of Command |

## Drill debriefing

Once the exercise has been completed, the officer in charge of the emergency party should conduct the debrief. This should cover:

- ☑ How the drill was carried out
- ☑ how to improve specific drill procedures
- ☑ any areas where more training is required
- ☑ equipment used, including any defects or necessary maintenance.

The purpose of any drill is to prepare for emergencies and this should be borne in mind when they are being organised. Drills are to be conducted as if there is an actual emergency and are to be varied to cover a range of situations. The Master should ensure that they are not allowed to degenerate into a periodic chore with no semblance of reality.

Crew are to be trained to carry out their own emergency duties efficiently and to know as much as is reasonably possible about other people's emergency duties. Drills should ensure that the vessel's crew reacts correctly to the particular circumstances devised for the exercise.

So far as weather conditions and time allow, exercises should be organised to incorporate as much realism as is safe and practical. Exercises should simulate a wide variety of hypothetical emergencies and contingencies, including:

☑ Fire(s) in:
- machinery spaces
- galley
- vehicle decks
- storerooms, workshops or lockers
- electrical equipment, wheelhouse or switchboards

☑ 'hampered' operations:
- loss of electrical power
- machinery failure
- loss of normal steering
- bridge or engine room out of action
- one side of the vessel inoperable/inaccessible
- senior officer/key personnel casualties

☑ damage control:
- collision
- hull holed after contact with quay, etc
- internal flooding following burst piping

☑ dangerous goods spillage

☑ entry into/rescue from dangerous spaces

☑ man overboard

☑ accident onboard:
- injury
- serious illness/death

☑ abandon ship.

Exercises should be designed to ensure that they provide crew training that includes, but is not limited to, the following:

☑ Use of survival craft and rescue boats in heavy weather

☑ survival techniques; hypothermia – effects and treatment

☑ first aid

☑ use of fire-fighting appliances, refilling of extinguishers

☑ use of breathing apparatus

- ☑ smoke/fume filled atmospheres
- ☑ search procedures within spaces
- ☑ control of passengers
- ☑ donning and use of fire-fighting and chemical suits
- ☑ entry into spaces on fire, opening of access to spaces
- ☑ effective fire-fighting techniques
- ☑ boundary cooling
- ☑ quick closing valves and remote stops.

Any single exercise could incorporate several of the above items. Consideration should be given to a pre-drill discussion on the purposes of the drill. Each drill should be followed by a debriefing session to analyse and reinforce particular points, provide explanations and consider suggestions for improved procedures. Every effort should be made to encourage a positive response to the exercises.

## 1.8    Training

Action Officer: Safety Officer

- The Safety Officer is responsible for producing the ship's training programme
- formal safety training should take place each week after emergency drills
- the Master should stand the navigational watch during this period
- all officers should be involved in this training
- the programme should provide a mixture of practical, video and classroom instruction
- the Safety Officer must keep a record of all instructions in a training record book.

Regular and realistic training is essential for the development and maintenance of emergency preparedness onboard, helping to foster a safety culture.

In an actual emergency situation, crew can become very afraid. However, experience has shown that crew members who regularly train and exercise in safety drills:

- Are less frightened
- do not panic
- respond in a controlled manner
- do exactly what they have been trained to do
- handle the situation much better than before the training.

If you wish your crew to perform competently in an emergency situation, you must remember that:

- There is no substitute for regular hands-on training and drills
- everybody onboard must be familiar with the response procedures in the event of an emergency
- emergency procedures for specific events will need to be followed

- a well trained crew with an ability to manage emergencies will prove invaluable should it be needed.

You must:

- ☑ Adhere strictly to the frequency of lifeboat, abandon ship, fire, ship security and other drills as prescribed by international laws and conventions
- ☑ use every opportunity to improve the routines of such drills
- ☑ conduct training as frequently as possible
- ☑ ensure that everybody attends any training provided
- ☑ have the training conducted and supervised by experienced officers, to show commitment from the highest level.

All drills should be followed by a debrief/wash-up session. Here important lessons can be learnt and implemented for the future.

Drills should be:

- ☑ As realistic as possible - this will help reduce fear in the event of an emergency situation
- ☑ carried out wearing full emergency equipment, where possible, to familiarise the crew with it
- ☑ recorded in the appropriate log book
- ☑ recorded in crew's individual training records (if applicable).

Safe training

Before conducting a training exercise, the equipment to be used should be thoroughly examined to ensure that it is safe to use. There have been many tragic accidents, particularly during lifeboat drills, and the utmost care must be exercised.

Training and drills may reveal a need for further training ashore and this should be reported to the company. Should you consider that additional training materials are required, the company should be informed.

Do not be too concerned if mistakes and errors are made during onboard training exercises and drills as this presents the best opportunity for the crew to learn from their mistakes and improve their skills.

Port State Control inspections often focus on familiarisation with lifeboat and fire drills. You should ensure that the crew are not only well trained in these drills, but also well trained in operating emergency fire generators and pumps and are familiar with emergency procedures concerning:

- Hot work incidents
- galley emergencies
- electrical incidents
- incinerator problems
- oil leaks and spills.

## 1.9 Port State Control and Other Safety Inspections

Action Officers: Safety Officer

☑ When any official safety inspector or coastguard arrives onboard, the Master and Chief Officer must be informed

☑ they should be shown to the ship's reception room, where the trading certificates must be presented

☑ all safety record books and checklists should be brought to the reception room for their inspection

☑ during any inspection, the inspectors must be accompanied by the Safety Officer. If he is not available, the senior Department Officer present must delegate another officer to accompany them

☑ once the inspection is completed, the Master and Chief Officer must be informed. A meeting will then be held in the ship's conference room/meeting room to discuss the inspection and any deficiencies found

☑ the Master must advise the company of the findings of the inspection.

## 1.10  Accident Prevention and New Crew Safety Induction

There are three reasons why we induct new personnel into the safety procedures of the ship. The first is because we have to. The second is to protect the ship and the company should the inductee have an accident. The third is that it makes sense. A ship hides many dangers for strangers or the unwary, especially those unfamiliar with its type. It is only by being shown around, and having the various safety procedures explained and safety equipment shown, that we can best prepare a newly joined crew member for integration into the ship's company.

Action Officers: Safety Officer, Chief Officer and 2nd Engineer Officer

- The Chief Officer and 2nd Engineer Officer are responsible for reviewing their individual department working practices and for ensuring that the safety induction is completed for joining crew
- they are responsible to the Safety Officer for ensuring that the safety familiarisation checklist is completed. The 2nd Engineer Officer is responsible for all the engine department personnel and the Chief Officer is responsible for all the deck and catering department personnel
- they are responsible for maintaining sufficient PPE (Personal Protective Equipment) in stock for their departments
- they are responsible for issuing and ensuring that crew members wear the correct PPE for the work being undertaken.

## 1.11 Accidents

In the event of any accident taking place, the following procedure should be adopted.

Action Officers: Safety Officer, OOW and Medical Officer

☑ Depending on the type of accident, the casualty will either be escorted to the ship's hospital or the ship's Medical Officer and stretcher party will be called to the scene. Any treatment given must be entered in the Medical Log Book

☑ if the casualty is suffering from any back or head injury, they should not be moved

☑ the Master must be informed

☑ the departmental Safety Officer for the area in which the accident occurred should start the accident investigation

☑ the OOW should maintain a log of all events and times throughout

☑ if the accident takes place in port:

- where a terminal worker is involved, the stevedore's office must be informed
- if the seriousness of the casualty warrants, contact the port emergency services with details of the accident and request medical services
- if the casualty is a member of the ship's company and requires shore medical treatment, this should be arranged immediately

☑ if the accident takes place at sea and is of a serious nature, prepare to contact the following:

- the Rescue Coordination Centre, Stavanger. INMARSAT A
- the International Medical Centre, Rome. SATCOM

☑ the Navigation Officer will lay courses for the nearest port or facility

☑ Safety Officers must complete the accident report for their areas of responsibility. This report must be completed as soon as possible after the accident

☑ a shipboard inquiry should be held by the Master, assisted by the Chief Engineer

- ☑ the company must be notified, using a method appropriate to the seriousness of the accident. The accident report should be faxed to the company
- ☑ on UK flagged ships or ships in UK waters, an MAIB report must be completed.

Slips, trips and falls are the major cause of personal injury onboard. The following precautions should be taken:

- ☑ Obstacles such as steps, sills, low overhead spaces, protruding handles, etc must be clearly marked
- ☑ the decks and alleyways of the vessel must be kept clean and free from any slippery substances
- ☑ hydraulic pipes on deck must be checked regularly to prevent leaking oil dripping onto the deck
- ☑ special attention must be paid to access areas to prevent slipping on ice in colder climates
- ☑ debris should be cleared from the deck
- ☑ defective anti-slip paint must be renewed
- ☑ sufficient lighting should always be provided
- ☑ handrails and grips must be in good condition
- ☑ appropriate warning signs should be provided where needed.

# 2 Pollution

As far as the Port or Flag State whose waters you are in are concerned, pollution is a most serious issue. Arrest and detention, of both ship and personnel, can follow and you can certainly expect delay to your vessel if an incident occurs in port. Pollution does not only come from oil. Even the smallest amount of garbage from your vessel can be perceived as pollution and heavy fines can be levied.

It is imperative that you can show that all procedures have been followed correctly and that your ship has done everything possible to minimise pollution.

One major problem for a ship is that, once oil has gone into the water, there is little the ship can do except rely on the shore clean-up facilities. The longer the shore takes to deal with the spill, the further it spreads.

## 2.1 Responsibilities

- The Chief Officer is responsible for all anti-pollution measures
- the Chief Officer is responsible for all anti-pollution equipment and stores
- the Chief Engineer is responsible for all bunkering procedures
- the Chief Engineer is team leader for the pollution clean-up team.

## 2.2    Garbage

Action Officer: Deck Officer keeping the 12 to 4 watch and designated Waste Disposal Officer (WDO)

### 2.2.1    Responsibilities

- ■ The WDO must keep all departments advised about the nature of the garbage disposal zone the ship is in
- ■ he must keep the Garbage Disposal Log Book
- ■ he should advise the Master, prior to arrival, about any garbage that will need to be disposed of by port facilities.

### 2.2.2    Garbage disposal

- ☑ When biodegradable garbage is ready for overboard disposal, the OOW on the bridge must be contacted for his authority
- ☑ the OOW must check that, in the area the ship is in, such disposal is permissible
- ☑ when garbage is thrown overboard, the OOW must enter the event's date, time and position in the Garbage Disposal Log Book
- ☑ non-biodegradable items must be placed in plastic bins
- ☑ prior to arrival in port, the WDO must advise the Master if any waste is to be disposed of ashore
- ☑ the Master should arrange for waste to be disposed of once in port. The WDO should obtain a receipt for this disposal, which will be filed by the Chief Officer.

### 2.2.3    Pollution from garbage

The disposal of ship's garbage, which is prohibited under MARPOL Annex V, is a criminal offence viewed in many countries in a similar manner to an act of oil pollution.

In ports with garbage disposal facilities, you should dispose of garbage in accordance with the vessel's Garbage Management Plan.

## 2.3   Bunkering

Action Officers: Chief Engineer, Chief Officer and OOW

- Prior to arrival in the bunkering port, the Chief Engineer must complete the company checklist and the oil spill contingency plan
- the Chief Officer must ensure that the Chief Engineer has a copy of the emergency contact list
- the Chief Engineer must check that all pollution precautions have been taken
- the Chief Engineer must ensure that all shipboard communications are in working order. He is responsible for communications with the shore or barge
- the Chief Officer must ensure that there is fire-fighting equipment in the vicinity of the bunkering position and that it is ready for use
- the Chief Officer must take all deck anti-pollution measures, such as blocking scuppers and preparing the pollution control equipment
- the deck department are responsible for making any bunkering barge fast alongside. They must assist with hoisting the bunkering pipe on board and must be responsible for the ladder to the barge
- the deck department must put up no smoking signs and rope off the bunkering position from shore workers
- the Chief Engineer must take fuel samples
- the Chief Engineer must agree and sign a receipt for fuel oil received, and advise the OOW when bunkering is complete
- the Chief Engineer must advise the Chief Officer of the amount received and the tanks that were filled.

## 2.3.1   Bunkering checklist (before transfer)

A precursor to a successful bunkering operation is the exchange of information prior to the operation. This should contain at least the following:

- ☑ Location, date and time of supply
- ☑ position where the bunkering is to occur
- ☑ acceptable weather and sea state conditions
- ☑ exact specification and amount of bunkers required
- ☑ is the bunker barge moored adequately?
- ☑ is there safe access from the ship to the bunker barge?
- ☑ are there new gaskets available for the bunker hose?
- ☑ is the connecting flange fitted with well-tightened bolts?
- ☑ is there a suitable webbing strop for the bunker hose?
- ☑ is the bunker hose(s) properly rigged?
- ☑ is there an effective watch in attendance on the ship/barge?
- ☑ are all pressure gauges, sampling devices and thermometers fitted securely?
- ☑ are save-alls available under each bunker hose? With plugs fitted?
- ☑ are all unused bunker connections properly blanked?
- ☑ are all scuppers effectively plugged?
- ☑ are vent flame screens on each bunker tank clear?
- ☑ is fire-fighting equipment available for immediate use?
- ☑ is oil spill equipment available for immediate use?
- ☑ is there an agreed communication system between own ship and the bunker barge?
- ☑ has an emergency stop procedure been agreed?
- ☑ are no smoking regulations in force on own ship and the bunker barge?
- ☑ has a bunker plan been agreed between own ship and the bunker barge?
- ☑ have all unused bunker valves been checked to confirm they are closed and means introduced to prevent accidental operation?
- ☑ have the tanks to be bunkered been gauged prior to the bunker transfer commencing?

☑    is there sufficient capacity in the bunker tanks on own vessel to receive the requested quantity without any bunker tank being filled beyond 95% capacity?

☑    are the sampling requirements and procedures for representative sampling before the commencement and during the bunkering operation agreed?

## 2.4    Oil Pollution from an Oil Tanker

Immediate action

☑    Sound emergency alarm.

Initial response

☑    Stop all cargo and/or bunkering operations
☑    close manifold valves
☑    switch air conditioning to recirculation or stop air intake to accommodation
☑    stop non-essential air intake fans to the engine room
☑    locate source of leakage and stop/reduce oil
☑    consult SOPEP plan
☑    consult MSDS/EMS guideline
☑    assess fire risk from release of flammable substances
☑    start fire pump
☑    commence clean-up procedures using absorbents and permitted solvents
☑    advise relevant parties (local authorities, coastal State, DPA/ company, P&I correspondent, etc).

Secondary response

☑    Reduce the oil level in the tank concerned by dropping oil into an empty or slack tank
☑    reduce the level of oil in tanks in the suspected area
☑    drain affected line to empty or slack tank
☑    reduce inert gas pressure to zero
☑    if the leakage is at the pumproom seavalve, relieve pressure on pipelines
☑    prepare pumps for transfer of oil to other tanks or to shore or lightering vessel
☑    prepare portable pumps if it is possible to transfer spilt oil to an empty tank
☑    consider pumping water into the leaking tank to create a water cushion and prevent further oil loss

- ☑ if the leakage is below the waterline, arrange divers for further investigation
- ☑ calculate stresses/stability. If necessary, request shore assistance
- ☑ transfer cargo or bunkers to alleviate high stability stresses
- ☑ stow residue from the clean-up operation carefully, prior to disposal.

## 2.4.1 Oil spilled on deck

When most of the free oil has been removed, and the risk of oil pollution has passed, onboard resources should turn to the clean-up operation.

Personnel involved in containment and clean-up operations may be at risk from a variety of hazards. The officer in charge of the operation should arrange for the following precautions to be taken to ensure that a safe working environment is maintained:

- ☑ The area must be continually checked for the presence of hydrocarbon and other suspected toxic gases (the MSDS will provide information regarding concentrations of specific toxic gases in a particular cargo)
- ☑ the boundaries of the clean-up site must be clearly indicated
- ☑ entry to the clean-up site must be controlled and access allowed only to those with appropriate PPE
- ☑ forced ventilation around the accommodation and machinery spaces must be controlled or stopped
- ☑ special precautions must be taken to prevent any sources of ignition, including static electricity
- ☑ fire-fighting parties and equipment should remain on standby
- ☑ surfaces that present a slipping hazard must be covered with sawdust or absorbent granules and hazard signs should be posted
- ☑ a designated area should be made available for personnel to shower and to change into clean clothing.

## 2.4.2   Pumproom spillage

Oil that is spilled in the pumproom from leaking pipelines may not present a pollution hazard, but it does present a personal health and safety hazard for those entering the pumproom. When a spill is suspected, entry into the pumproom must be treated as though it were an enclosed entry into a cargo oil tank. The pumproom entry permit must be cancelled.

The initial strategy should be as follows:

- ☑ Stop cargo operations
- ☑ evacuate personnel from the pumproom
- ☑ withdraw pumproom entry permit
- ☑ close all remotely operated valves
- ☑ monitor % LEL using fixed and portable instruments (in the case of portable instruments, no metal probes should be used)
- ☑ prepare the bilge pump or the pump designated for bilge pumping duty and set the lines to transfer to a suitable cargo oil tank
- ☑ if the pumproom bilge alarm has been activated and/or oil is being drawn into the pumproom extraction vents, consider changing over to the high extraction vents.

Further action depends on the situation.

### 2.4.3   Oil pollution of unknown origin

If oil is detected in the water near the vessel, and is not due to a collision or grounding, steps must be taken to determine the source by:

- ☑ Taking surface samples, using a purpose designed surface sampler or a wipe or clean rag attached to a sounding rod, to determine the type of oil for comparison. At least two samples should be taken, clearly labelled with the position they were taken from with respect to the tanker, the geographical position, date and time
- ☑ take a set of ullages and soundings of fuel and cargo tanks and compare them with the last daily record of soundings and ullages
- ☑ to identify any possible source, sequentially shut down all possible systems that discharge overboard.

## 2.5    Other Sources of Pollution

You should familiarise yourself with items of pollution documented in your company's SMS and with the provisions of MARPOL 73/78 (plus latest amendments).

### 2.5.1   Sewage

Stricter regulations to prevent pollution of the sea by sewage have been implemented. MARPOL 73/78 Annex IV details the regulations for the Prevention of Pollution by Sewage from Ships.

### 2.5.2   Ballast water

Ballast water is one of the major sources of the spread of harmful aquatic organisms and pathogens to new areas.

The 'Guidelines for the Control and Management of Ship's Ballast Water to Minimize the Transfer of Harmful Aquatic Organisms and Pathogens' (IMO Resolution 868) were adopted by the IMO in December 1997.

To control the invasion of aquatic organisms and pathogens, the US introduced the 'US National Invasive Species Act of 1996'. This:

- Amended existing regulations for the Great Lakes
- established voluntary ballast water management guidelines for US waters
- established mandatory reporting for vessels entering US waters.

If trading to the US or countries where ballast water regulations are in force, you should:

- ☑ Ask the agent before entering the Exclusive Economic Zone (200 nautical miles) how you can comply with the country's ballast water requirements
- ☑ ensure you are familiar with all relevant local and international requirements in force.

You should be aware that certain countries have imposed significant fines on vessels discharging ballast water in their jurisdictions without the correct procedures in place.

### 2.5.3 Air pollution

In April 1999, the European Union issued Directive 1999/32, which came into force on 1 July 2002, stating that a sulphur cap is in place on inland use of middle distillate fuels, with a similar cap placed on the marine use of such products. This Directive placed a sulphur limit on all grades of fuel and now includes a sulphur cap of 1.5% by mass on marine diesel oil (MDO), placing restrictions on its use, particularly for transit between EU ports.

Exhaust gases from any combustion engine, including ships' engines, contribute to these emissions and can be reduced, improving the efficiency of the combustion of fuel oils.

Visible air pollution by soot from the ship's funnel may still occur and the consequences are often far reaching. Soot can be carried for miles on the wind and result in damage to property. Annex VI of MARPOL covers air pollution and came into force in May 2005.

## 2.6    Evidence to be Collected in the Event of a Pollution Incident

In addition to maintaining a continuous record of all events, the following evidence must be collected.

### Description of the incident

- ☑ Date and time of pollution
- ☑ nature of the pollution
- ☑ ongoing operation at the time the pollution occurred
- ☑ estimation of the amount spilled
- ☑ ship's position
- ☑ weather conditions (particularly wind direction and force)
- ☑ tide and current
- ☑ draught of the vessel.

### If pollution occurred at sea

- ☑ Courses on charts
- ☑ speed and engine setting
- ☑ position log and distances to the nearest coastline.

### Description of the ongoing operation at the time of the pollution

- ☑ Type of operation
- ☑ time the operation commenced and pertinent facts
- ☑ details of the persons involved (and responsibilities) on the ship and/or bunker barge.

### Details of other companies involved in the pollution

- ☑ Name and contact details
- ☑ names, details and duties of their personnel involved in the operation

- ☑ name of bunker barge
- ☑ if the pollution occurred during bunkering:
  - • had procedures been agreed, in particular regarding commencement, rate of flow, interruptions
  - • how communications were maintained
- ☑ any difficulties in communicating or conducting the operation.

## Damage caused by the pollution

- ☑ Description of the pollution
- ☑ location and extent of the pollution.

# 3 Medical

We are not trained medical attendants, but we are first aiders with a smattering of knowledge gained many years ago, often with no refresher training. Having said that, it is surprising how much general knowledge you will pick up as a Master.

The officer who is designated as the Medical Officer may have more knowledge than you or may have far less. Either way, in the event of anything serious, you will have to be in attendance.

With all treatment, regardless of perceived unimportance, a full record is essential, not just for you but for the patient, the company and the P&I Club.

## 3.1 Responsibilities

Responsible Officer: Master

Action Officer: Deck Officer keeping the 12 to 4 watch, designated ship's Medical Officer

- The ship's Medical Officer is responsible for the onboard medical treatment of all the ship's company. He is also responsible for maintaining their medical files
- he is responsible for the care and maintenance of all medical equipment, such as the respirator. He must ensure that any crew who are to use this equipment are instructed on how to do so
- he is responsible for the maintenance of the first aid lockers in the galley, engine room, deck office and on the bridge. He will ensure that the emergency first aid party pack is complete
- the cleanliness and preparedness of the hospital and dispensary are the Medical Officer's responsibility, and they should never be used as a store or cabin

- the Medical Officer will maintain the Medical Log Book, which must be available in the hospital for inspection by the Master
- the dangerous drugs list is compiled by the Medical Officer
- all medical stores and supplies are his responsibility
- while on passage, if a medicine expires, it will need to be declared as such in any customs declaration. Any surplus medicines not recorded in the medical stores list may arouse suspicions with authorities and may have serious consequences
- access to the medicine locker should be restricted to authorised personnel only, in accordance with the company's or the Flag State's rules
- no crew member should be allowed to possess private medicines without the Master being notified. The crew should be requested to compile a list of any private medicines carried onboard. Possession of undeclared private medicines may in some countries constitute a breach of customs or other regulations, with the possibility of a fine being imposed on the Master and the individual crew member. If a crew member has been prescribed medication, the original or a certified copy of the prescription should be carried, together with the medicine
- the presence of any serious infection may lead you to request the company to arrange for repatriation of the crew member concerned.

## 3.2    Treatment

Action Officers: Ship's Medical Officer and Heads of Department

The procedure for treatment should be as follows:

- ☑ The dispensary must be opened for treatment by contacting the Medical Officer
- ☑ any treatment given should be logged. This will evidence proper medical care and will demonstrate to any authorities how medicine abuse is being prevented
- ☑ should the Medical Officer have any doubt about a diagnosis or the treatment to give, the Master should be consulted
- ☑ if the Medical Officer decides that shore treatment is required, the appropriate medical treatment form must be completed
- ☑ the Medical Officer should advise the Chief Engineer or the Chief Officer if a member of their department needs to be sent ashore for medical treatment. If possible, a convenient time should be arranged for the patient to attend the doctor
- ☑ the Medical Officer must advise the Master of any shore treatment that is required so that the Master can arrange this through the agents
- ☑ on the patient's return to the ship, the medical form must be collected and a copy sent to the company
- ☑ if any patient is placed off duty, either by the ship's Medical Officer or by the shore medical authorities, the Head of the Department and the Master must be advised immediately
- ☑ any patient who is off duty must be checked daily by the Medical Officer, who will then report daily to the Master
- ☑ if hospitalisation or repatriation is recommended by the shore medical authorities, the Master, agent and company must be advised immediately
- ☑ the Head of Department will arrange the patient's personal effects to be landed
- ☑ the Administration Officer (Master) should arrange for the patient's documents to be landed
- ☑ the Master must arrange for the patient's pay off

- ☑ should the Medical Officer be unavailable, a Head of Department may place a crew member temporarily off duty until the Medical Officer becomes available
- ☑ any injury or illness which prevents a seafarer from working for more than 3 days should be reported to the MAIB if on a UK vessel or any vessel in UK waters.

## 3.3    Injury, Illness or Death

### 3.3.1  Injury

In the event of personal injury, crew illness or death, your P&I Club
should be contacted at the earliest opportunity.

**Action to be taken**

- ☑ Refer to any Emergency Action Plans/SMS
- ☑ provide medical care using the most skilled medic onboard
- ☑ where risk of internal injury may occur, do not move the casualty until an experienced medic is in attendance
- ☑ obtain medical advice from ashore
- ☑ at sea, consider deviating for medical assistance
- ☑ in port, call an ambulance and the local P&I correspondent
- ☑ notify the company and your P&I Club
- ☑ maintain a record of all communications
- ☑ submit an MAIB report as appropriate.

If a crew member is hospitalised and is unable to return to the vessel,
you should:

**Collection of evidence**

- ☑ Ensure the area is not disturbed until photographs and videos have been taken as evidence
- ☑ note the date/time that each photograph/video was taken
- ☑ if no camera is available, make drawings/sketches showing the location/position in which the person was found
- ☑ record all communications concerning the event
- ☑ retain wires, shackles or tools that may have caused the injury, mark or label as appropriate and store in a safe place.

**Further evidence to be collected**

- ☑ Name, sex and duties of the person concerned
- ☑ date and time (ship's and UTC) when the accident occurred
- ☑ ship's position

- ☑ weather conditions
- ☑ vessel movement
- ☑ illumination levels at the time, eg daylight, darkness, artificial light
- ☑ exact location on the vessel and the conditions in that area
- ☑ work activity the person was engaged in and the time it began
- ☑ hours of work and rest records, any indictions of fatigue
- ☑ permit to work/risk assessment for the task
- ☑ PPE in use at the time
- ☑ witness details
- ☑ details of hospital/doctor who administered treatment
- ☑ medical treatment given
- ☑ any indications of intoxication or drug abuse
- ☑ detailed statements.

### 3.3.2 Illness

In the event of illness of a crew member or passenger, a subsequent claim could be issued for negligence by the person that was taken ill. Adherence to agreed company procedures will limit the possibility of this arising.

**Action to be taken**

- ☑ Provide medical care using the most skilled medic onboard
- ☑ obtain medical advice from ashore
- ☑ at sea, consider deviating for medical assistance
- ☑ in port, call an ambulance and the local P&I correspondent
- ☑ notify the company and your P&I Club
- ☑ maintain a record of all communications
- ☑ submit an MAIB report as appropriate.

If a crew member is hospitalised and is unable to return to the vessel, you should:

- ☑ Make a record of and pack all the personal effects of the crew member, preferably with two officers as witnesses. The effects should be delivered to the care of the ship's agent to arrange for transfer to the hospital
- ☑ ask the P&I correspondent to notify local consulate of the crew member
- ☑ request a replacement for the crew member.

### 3.3.3   Death

In the event of a death onboard, there will not generally a doctor available to examine the deceased and determine the likely cause of death. In the event of a death by accident or unnatural causes, a post-mortem will almost certainly be required by the local/national police authorities once the body is landed ashore.

**Actions**

- ☑ Seek medical advice to establish with certainty that the person is dead. Refer to the Ship Master's Medical Guide
- ☑ determine how best to preserve the corpse. There may be 'body bags' in the medical stores and the corpse should be kept cool by keeping it in the refrigerated stores
- ☑ if a means of preserving the corpse is not available, seek guidance from your company and P&I Club concerning:
  - • deviating to land the body ashore (if deviating, notify the company and P&I Club as this will allow them to assist and notify the appropriate authorities)
  - • burial at sea
- ☑ if in port, request both a doctor and the local P&I correspondent immediately. This will allow them to assist in notification to the appropriate authorities
- ☑ all medical related messages should be recorded
- ☑ ensure that the next of kin are notified
- ☑ make a record of and pack all the personal effects of the deceased, preferably with two officers as witnesses. The

      personal items should be delivered to the care of the ship's agent who will arrange for return to the next of kin
☑ ask the P&I correspondent to notify the local consulate of the deceased
☑ request a replacement crew member.

## Collection of Evidence

☑ Ensure the area is not disturbed until photographs and/or videos have been taken as evidence
☑ note the date/time that each photograph/video was taken
☑ if no camera is available, make drawings/sketches showing the location and position in which the person was found
☑ record all communications concerning the event
☑ evidence such as wires, shackles and tools that may have caused the death should be collected, marked, labelled and retained in a safe place.

## Further evidence to be collected

☑ Name, sex and duties of the deceased
☑ date and time (ship's and UTC) when the death occurred
☑ ship's position
☑ weather conditions
☑ vessel movement
☑ illumination levels at the time, eg daylight, darkness, artificial light
☑ exact location on the vessel and the conditions in that area
☑ work activity the deceased was engaged in and the time it began
☑ hours of work and rest records, any indications of fatigue
☑ permit to work/risk assessment for the task
☑ PPE in use at the time of death
☑ witness details
☑ details of hospital/doctor who attended the deceased
☑ medical treatment given
☑ any indications of intoxication or drug abuse
☑ detailed statements from any witnesses to the event.

## 3.4    Drugs and Alcohol

You should ensure that the company's drugs and alcohol policy is strictly enforced. Any deviations may have serious consequences for the safe and secure operation of the vessel and crew.

### 3.4.1    General

Comprehensive information should be provided to the crew on:

- The drugs and alcohol policy of the company
- the possibility that the vessel could be used for smuggling drugs and the consequences of any of the ship's crew giving support to drug dealers
- the consequences should a crew member be found with drugs for personal use (ie criminal prosecution).

### 3.4.2    Drug use onboard

You should make it very clear to the crew that the possession or use of drugs has an impact on the safety and security of the vessel and crew and is likely to lead to instant dismissal, with all associated costs of repatriation and replacement deducted from the individual's salary.

### 3.4.3    Measures to prevent drug smuggling

The cover provided by your P&I Club may be void if the vessel is found to be smuggling drugs.

The following basic measures, that can be taken in port or in an anchorage, will assist:

- ☑ Prepare a detailed search list for drugs
- ☑ regular searches, based on this list, should be completed prior to and upon sailing from any port with a reputation for drug smuggling
- ☑ at night, illuminate the exterior of the vessel, adjacent pier and water areas

☑ all doors to the accommodation and store rooms should be locked and those that are not required during the stay should be sealed

☑ any compartments that could be used for smuggling or concealment of drugs should be secured and sealed

☑ any areas of the ship that cannot be sealed should be accessible to authorised personnel only

☑ employ a gangway security system 24 hours a day

☑ any empty containers should be locked and sealed and the serial number of the seal noted.

### 3.4.4 If drugs are found

The company and the P&I insurer should be contacted immediately. Actions should be taken and evidence collected to protect the company and the crew members.

Before the authorities arrive:

☑ The drugs must not be touched

☑ photograph/video the location where the drugs were found

☑ ensure the area is left untouched

☑ seal off the area to prevent any unauthorised access.

If any broken seals are discovered, they should be recorded in the log book and on the bill of lading, noting the seal numbers.

### 3.4.5 Alcohol

You should make it clear to the crew that any deviation from the company's alcohol policy will have serious personal consequences, including possible instant dismissal.

While moderate consumption of alcohol is considered a social activity, excessive amounts can seriously affect the safety and security of the vessel and her crew.

Your rights to carry out breath or blood tests will be subject to the regulations of the Flag State and the terms of the crew contracts of employment.

# 4 Navigation

The passage of the ship on the seas, while not your main function as Master, is the one of most concern to you. The general day to day navigation is, under your supervision, in the hands of the officers of the deck department. As the ship gets close to land, your attention to it will grow and by the time you are in busy traffic areas it will absorb all of your time and often your direct control.

The Navigation Officer should know what you expect of him and what his sphere of responsibility is. However, all Masters are different and so you must tell him how you expect the navigation of the ship to be carried out.

## 4.1 Responsibilities

Responsible Officer: Master
Action Officer: Officer keeping the 12 to 4 watch and designated ship's Navigation Officer

The Navigation Officer is responsible for:

- The upkeep of all navigation and bridge publications
- all charts and their corrections
- charterer's and owner's log abstracts
- passage planning
- routine navigational messages
- correct functioning of all bridge equipment
- all the ship's stationery requirements
- all noon and owner's/charterer's position reports
- maintenance of all bridge equipment
- all ETAs to port/pilot and agents.

## 4.2   Passage Planning

- When the ship is advised of its next employment, the Navigation Officer must check that all the necessary charts are on board and corrected with the latest available information
- he must check the port of destination for draught and navigational dangers and consult with the Master if he has any doubt as to the safety of the port or passage into the port
- he must arrange for a consultation time with the Master to discuss the type of sailing and general directions for passage. On this basis, he will prepare the passage, advising the Master once it is completed
- after the Master has approved the passage, the Navigation Officer must prepare a list of courses and distances and a detailed voyage plan
- if required, prior to arrival, the pilots at the destination port will be asked to fax the port approach plan to the ship.

## 4.3   Communications

The Navigation Officer will issue, as required, the following navigational messages:

- AMVER
- National Ship Reporting System messages
- Routine charter position reports
- Routine company position reports.

### 4.3.1  GMDSS Log Book entries

The following is a brief summary of what should be recorded in the GMDSS Log Book:

- ☑ A summary of any distress, urgency or safety communications received
- ☑ ship's position, at least once per day
- ☑ condition of the radio equipment
- ☑ details of personnel assigned the responsibility for sending distress alerts
- ☑ training on the use of the radio equipment to relevant crew members
- ☑ pre-sailing checks to ensure that the GMDSS station is in working order
- ☑ results of the testing of the DSC distress and safety radio equipment at least once a week. This should be by means of a test call
- ☑ monthly testing of SART, EPIRB and GMDSS VHF radios
- ☑ results of the testing of the distress and safety radio equipment at least once a day (by means of a test without radiating any signal)
- ☑ daily test of the batteries (on-load and off-load)
- ☑ weekly hydrometer test of the batteries
- ☑ results of the monthly integrity check of each battery and its connections
- ☑ the Master is to sign the GMDSS Log Book once per day.

## 4.4    Equipment Maintenance

☑    If there is any malfunction of bridge equipment, the Navigation Officer should issue a repair chit to the department or officer concerned with the repair

☑    he must advise the Master of any equipment malfunction

☑    once the repair has been carried out, he should let the Master know

☑    should shore assistance be required, he should advise the Master, who will consult with the officer responsible for the maintenance of the equipment

☑    the company should be kept informed if it is necessary.

## 4.5    Emergency Situation Procedures

Be careful of emergency situation procedures - like most plans, things start to unravel shortly after beginning and the more elaborate they are the faster they unravel. Keep it simple. Remember that you are the Master and there to deal with the situation, not to just repeat what a book says. Any procedure is purely guidance to remind you what to consider during an emergency. In the heat of the moment, it is easy to forget something that, while not immediately essential to the immediate situation, is still important to your actions overall.

Finally, it is useful to have each situation on a separate card in an easily reachable box in the front of the bridge, allowing it to be quickly retrieved and read without having to search through a book.

Responsible Officer: The Master
Action Officer: The Chief Officer

- The emergency procedure cards should be read by all officers
- the Chief Officer must ensure that each weekly drill includes an emergency procedure
- an emergency procedure should be discussed at each safety meeting
- all emergency procedures should be reviewed at a periodic meeting of the Master and the Safety Officers, together with the heads of department. If it is felt that changes are required that will affect the company SMS, the Master should advise the company of this.

## 4.6   Flags

Flags are an affectionate anachronism that, with the minimum manning of most ships, tend to be neglected more and more. It would be easier to paint the nationality on the ship's side and leave it at that, but I feel that position is some way off. Until then, we must wear our flags. The flags do, to an extent, reflect the ship, so tatty dirty ones display a certain message about you and your attitude. If you are going to wear the flags then wear them correctly. If everyone remembered to take them down at night and in bad weather, they would certainly stay in better condition longer!

Action Officers: Deck Officer keeping the 8 to 12 watch and OOW

- ☑ Once the ship has been advised of its next intended voyage, the flags required for this voyage must be checked and new ones ordered if necessary
- ☑ all flags and halyards should be kept in a good state of repair. The Chief Officer will arrange crew as required by the Action Officer for this
- ☑ prior to arrival in port, the required flags should be labelled and put out ready for use.

## 4.7    Helicopter Transfer - Planned Operation

Helicopter operations are now commonplace on many vessels and are used for a variety of tasks such as pilot transfer, delivery of stores, emergency medical evacuations and crew transfer. As with all frequent operations, as it becomes common place, the various precautions tend to decline. It is only when an accident happens that the essential need for these precautions becomes apparent.

Helicopter operations have the potential of being one of the most dangerous operations taking place on a ship, with the possibility of an accident always present. If this occurs, the precautions taken by the ship and the readiness of the deck party in dealing with an incident will determine the outcome.

The Helicopter Landing Officer is in charge of the landing operations at all times, from when the helicopter makes its final approach until it has taken off and is clear of the ship. He must at all times be in direct contact with the bridge and be able to direct the helicopter by light signals and or communications throughout the operation. At any time, should he not be satisfied as to the safety of the operation, he has the authority to abort the operation and wave off the helicopter. He should have a signal torch that can show red for wave-off and green for safe approach.

It is imperative that all the deck party remain upwind of the operations area and a good distance away. Those not immediately involved with the operation should, if possible, be sheltered. A helicopter accident can scatter pieces of rotor blade and burning debris over a wide area.

The ship's emergency party should be regularly drilled in dealing with such an emergency.

### 4.7.1  Prior to helicopter operations

The following information should be provided to the helicopter operators or your agent:

- ☑ ETA
- ☑ ship's speed and course
- ☑ present weather conditions, including visibility
- ☑ present pitches, roll and heave
- ☑ diameter of landing zone or winch area
- ☑ VHF frequencies to be used
- ☑ any locating aids, such as non-directional beacons.

### 4.7.2  On helicopter approach

- ☑ Establish VHF contact
- ☑ confirm the vessel's speed and course
- ☑ confirm pitch, roll and heave
- ☑ confirm wind direction, force and visibility
- ☑ if safe, set course and speed as requested by the helicopter
- ☑ confirm the landing area is clear for landing or winch area is clear for operations
- ☑ advise the pilot if the landing area is wet and taking water (in exceptional circumstances, to avoid skidding, netting can be laid on the landing area. This should only be done after discussion with the pilot).

### 4.7.3  Deck preparation

- ☑ A windsock should be hoisted where the approaching helicopter will have a clear view. At night, this should be illuminated
- ☑ ensure the area of operations is clear of loose equipment and debris. Cargo residue should be washed down
- ☑ ensure that all rigging in the area is secure and clear of the operations area
- ☑ the whole area should initially be illuminated, especially masts, aerials and rigging in the vicinity. Any lighting that could interfere with the helicopter pilot's vision should be shielded

☑ the bridge should ensure that personnel are standing by to control the lighting when required to do so by the helicopter pilot

☑ the fire party should be standing by with the following equipment:

- fire hoses connected, fire pump on and line pressurised, foam nozzle fitted and foam container standing by
- axe
- crowbar
- hacksaw
- boltcutters
- ladder
- torches (at night).

### 4.7.4  PPE

The helideck operations party should wear the following:

☑ Flame retardant overalls and gloves (hose party fire suits)
☑ helmets with visors
☑ safety boots
☑ ear protectors.

## 4.8 MGN 315 (Keeping a Safe Navigational Watch on Merchant Vessels)

*This notice gives information and guidance on the keeping and maintaining of a safe navigational watch in accordance with the requirements of STCW 95 and its associated code (STCW Code).*

*The areas that this notice covers are:*

*General application for Masters and officers in charge of a navigational watch;*
*Fitness for duty;*
*Performing the navigational watch;*
*Watch arrangements, handing over the watch and taking over the watch;*
*Maintaining a safe look-out and relationship with the look-out;*
*Restricted visibility, safe speed, stopping distance and vessel at anchor;*
*Certification.*

*Available from the Publications Department, International Maritime Organization, 4 Albert Embankment, London SE1 7SR*

### 1.0 *Introduction*

1.1 *This notice contains guidance for officers in charge of a navigational watch, which Masters are expected to supplement as they consider appropriate. It is essential that officers of the watch (OOW) appreciate that the proper performance of their duties is necessary in the interests of the safety of life and property at sea and the prevention of pollution to the marine environment.*

1.2 *It is the responsibility of Masters, and companies owning or operating UK registered seagoing vessels, to ensure that the principles applying to the keeping of a safe watch, as detailed in STCW 95 are followed.*

1.3 *The Master shall not be constrained by the shipowner, charterer or any person from taking any decision which, in the Master's professional judgment, is necessary for safe navigation. It is the duty of the Master of every vessel to ensure that watchkeeping arrangements are adequate for maintaining a safe navigational watch at all times.*

1.4 *The International Chamber of Shipping (ICS) Bridge Procedures Guide is established as the principle guide to best watchkeeping practice and includes additional guidance on bridge resource management and the conduct of the bridge team including the use of passage planning, integrated electronic navigation systems and the use of GMDSS.*

1.5 *This notice, which should be read in conjunction with STCW 95 and ICS Bridge Procedures Guide, highlights the Maritime and Coastguard Agency (MCA) concerns and interpretations with respect to what constitutes the 'Keeping of a Safe Navigational Watch' in the light of recent maritime accidents and incidents.*

1.6 *The Annex to this notice lists relevant publications.*

2.0 *General*

2.1 *The OOW is the Master's representative and is primarily responsible at all times for the safe navigation of the vessel and for complying with the International Regulations for Preventing Collisions At Sea (ColRegs).*

2.2 *It is of special importance that the OOW ensures that at all times an efficient look-out is maintained and that ColRegs are complied with.*

2.3 *Officers and Masters are reminded that the vessel must at all times proceed at a safe speed.*

2.4 *The vessel's engines are at the disposal of the OOW and there should be no hesitation in using them in case of need. Where possible, timely notice of intended variations of engine speed should be given to the duty engineer. The OOW should know the handling characteristics of the vessel including the stopping distance, and should appreciate that other vessels may have different handling characteristics.*

2.5 *Officers in charge of a navigational watch are responsible for navigating the vessel safely during their periods of duty with particular concerns for avoiding collision and stranding. The OOW shall also be aware of the serious effects of operational or accidental pollution of the marine environment and shall take all possible precautions to prevent such pollution.*

2.6 *Masters, owners and operators are reminded that the MCA considers it dangerous and irresponsible for the OOW to act as sole look-out during periods of darkness or restricted visibility.*

2.7 *The factors to be considered before the dedicated bridge look-out can be dispensed with are detailed in paragraph 8.3. It is implicit in STCW 95 that at all times when a ship is underway a separate dedicated look-out must be kept in addition to the OOW.*

### 3.0 Fitness for Duty

3.1 *The Merchant Shipping (Hours of Work) Regulations 2002 (the Regulations) apply to all seafarers employed or engaged in any capacity on board a seagoing vessel and includes officers and ratings assigned to bridge watchkeeping duties.*

3.2 *In summary, and unless covered by an exception, the Regulations provide for a minimum of 10 hours rest in any 24 hour period and 77 hours in any seven day period. Hours of rest may be divided into no more than two periods, one of which should be at least six hours long, and the intervals in between should not exceed 14 hours.*

3.3 *The watch system shall be such that the efficiency of watchkeeping personnel is not impaired by fatigue. The Master shall take into account the quality and quantity of rest taken by the watchkeepers when determining fitness for duty.*

3.4 *It is the overall responsibility of the Master and the responsibility of every watchkeeping officer and rating to ensure that they are sufficiently rested prior to taking over a navigational watch. It is the responsibility of the owner or operator to ensure that the vessel is manned with a sufficient number of personnel so* that a safe navigational watch can be maintained at all times by appropriately qualified and rested personnel in all foreseeable circumstances.

3.5 In circumstances where the Regulations cannot be met there should be established procedures and contingencies in place to ensure that the vessel is brought to or remains in a place of safety until a safe navigational watch can be established. In some circumstances this may require delay to a vessel's departure.

3.6 Watchkeepers should ensure they remain alert by moving around frequently and ensuring good ventilation. Marine Accident Investigation Branch (MAIB) reports have shown that it is all too easy to fall asleep, especially while sitting down in an enclosed wheelhouse.

3.7 The OOW shall be free from the effects of alcohol and any other substance, including prescription drugs or other medication that may have a detrimental effect on the officer's judgments.

## 4.0 Performing the Navigational Watch

4.1 The officer of the navigational watch shall:

- Keep the watch on the bridge
- in no circumstances leave the bridge until properly relieved by an appropriate officer
- continue to be responsible for the safe navigation of the vessel despite the presence of the Master on the bridge until informed specifically that the Master has assumed the con and this is mutually understood
- notify the Master when in any doubt as to what action to take in the interests of safety
- continue to be responsible for the safe navigation of the vessel despite the presence of a pilot on board
- if in any doubt as to the pilot's actions or intentions, seek clarification from the pilot; if doubt still exists, they should notify the Master immediately and take whatever action is necessary until the Master arrives

- ■   *not undertake any other duties that would interfere or compromise the keeping of a safe navigational watch*
- ■   *ensure there are no distractions caused by the use of domestic radios, cassettes, CD players, personal computers, television sets, mobile phones, etc*
- ■   *have available at all times, the services of a qualified helmsman*
- ■   *in areas of high traffic density, in conditions of restricted visibility and in all hazardous navigational situations ensure the vessel is in hand steering*
- ■   *keep in mind that the perceptions of watchkeeping officers on different types and sizes of vessels may vary considerably when assessing a close quarter situation and the time in which avoiding action should be taken*
- ■   *keep a proper record during the watch on the movement and activities relating to the navigation of the vessel*
- ■   *station a person to steer the vessel and to put the steering into manual control in good time to allow any potentially hazardous situation to be dealt with in a safe manner. Officers are further reminded that when the vessel is in automatic steering it is highly dangerous to allow a situation to develop to the point where the OOW is without assistance and has to break the continuity of the look-out in order to take emergency action*
- ■   *use the radar at all times in areas of high traffic density and whenever restricted visibility is encountered or expected and shall have due regard to its limitations. Radar should be available for use at all times to enable the officers to use the equipment in clear weather so as to fully appreciate the limitations of the equipment*
- ■   *at sufficiently frequent intervals during the watch check the vessel's position, course and speed using all appropriate navigational aids and means necessary to ensure that the vessel follows the planned track*
- ■   *take fixes at frequent intervals. These fixes shall be carried out by more than one method whenever circumstances allow. The largest scale chart on board, suitable for the area and corrected with the latest available information*

shall be used. This includes local navigation warnings, and temporary and preliminary notices to mariners

Mariners are also reminded of the requirement to use the latest editions of all supporting navigational publications such as charts, list of lights, list of radio signals, pilot books etc. Such publications should be fully corrected.

## 5.0 *Watch Arrangements*

5.1 *The composition of a navigational watch should comprise one (or more) qualified officers supported by appropriately qualified ratings. The actual number of officers and ratings on watch at a particular time will depend on the prevailing circumstances and conditions.*

5.2 *At no time shall the bridge be left unmanned without a qualified watchkeeping officer.*

5.3 *Factors to be taken into account when composing a bridge watch:*

- *Fatigue*
- *weather conditions and visibility*
- *proximity of navigational hazards which may make it necessary for the officer in charge of the watch to carry out additional navigational duties*
- *use and operational condition of navigational aids*
- *whether the vessel is fitted with automatic steering*
- *whether there are radio duties to be performed*
- *unmanned machinery space (UMS) alarms, controls and indicators provided on the bridge, procedures for their use and limitations*
- *any unusual demands on the navigational watch that may arise as a result of special operational circumstances.*

*In circumstances where a single man bridge is considered permissible support personnel should be readily and immediately available should assistance be required. There should be an established and continuously available means of communications for the watchkeeper to summon such assistance at all times.*

### 6.0 Handing Over the Watch

6.1 *The OOW shall:*

- ■ *Ensure that the members of the relieving watch are fully capable of performing their duties*
- ■ *ensure that the vision of the relieving watch is fully adjusted to the light conditions*
- ■ *ensure that all standing orders and the Master's night orders are fully understood.*

6.2 *The OOW shall not hand over the watch:*

- ■ *If there is reason to believe that the relieving officer is not capable of carrying out the watchkeeping duties effectively, in which case the Master should be notified*
- ■ *when a manoeuvre is in progress until such action has been completed.*

### 7.0 Taking Over the Watch

7.1 *The relieving officer shall:*

- ■ *Prior to taking over the watch verify the vessel's estimated or true position*
- ■ *confirm the vessel's intended track, course and speed*
- ■ *note any dangers to navigation expected to be encountered during the watch*
- ■ *be aware of prevailing and predicted tides, currents, weather, visibility and the effect of these factors upon course and speed*
- ■ *note any errors in gyro and magnetic compasses*
- ■ *note the status of all bridge equipment*
- ■ *note the settings of bridge/engine controls and manning of engine room*

- *be aware of the presence and movement of vessels in sight or known to be in the vicinity*
- *give watchkeeping personnel all appropriate instructions and information which will ensure the keeping of a safe navigational watch, including maintenance of a proper look-out.*

## 8.0 *Look-out*

8.1 *The ColRegs require that every vessel shall at all times maintain a proper look-out by sight and hearing as well as by all available means appropriate in the prevailing circumstances and conditions so as to make a full appraisal of the situation and of risk of collision.*

8.2 *The look-out must be able to give full attention to the keeping of a proper look-out and no other duties shall be undertaken that could interfere with that task. The duties of the look-out and helmsman are separate and the helmsman should not be considered to be a look-out except in small vessels where an unobstructed all round view is provided at the steering position and there is no impairment of night vision or other impediment to the keeping of a proper look-out.*

8.3 *In certain circumstances of clear daylight conditions the Master may consider that the OOW may be the sole look-out. On each occasion the Master should ensure that:*

- *The prevailing situation has been carefully assessed and it has been established without a doubt that it is safe to do so*
- *full account has been taken of all the relevant factors including but not limited to:*
  - *state of the weather*
  - *visibility*
  - *traffic density*
  - *proximity of dangers to navigation*
  - *the attention necessary when navigating in or near traffic separation scemes*

- *design and layout of the bridge*
- *arcs of visibility*
- *radar equipment fitted and their limitations with respect to navigation*
- *other duties that the officer may have to engage in and which could be a distraction from the keeping of a proper look-out such as:*
    - *operation of GMDSS and other communications equipment such as cell phones and email systems*
    - *navigational maintenance such as completion of logs and other record keeping and correction of charts and publications*
    - *routine testing and maintenance of bridge equipment.*

*In any event, an OOW acting as sole look-out should always be able to fully perform both the duties of a look-out and those of keeping a safe navigational watch. Assistance must be immediately available to be summoned to the bridge when any change in the situation so requires.*

8.4 *It is of special importance that at all times the officer in charge of the navigational watch ensures that a proper look-out is maintained. In vessels with a separate chartroom the officer in charge of the navigational watch may visit the chartroom, when essential, for a short period for the necessary performance of navigational duties, but shall first ensure that it is safe to do so and that a proper look-out is maintained.*

9.0 *Relationship Between the OOW and Look-out*

9.1 *The OOW should consider the look-out as an integral part of the Bridge Team and utilise the look-out to the fullest extent.*

9.2 *As a way of fully engaging the look-out's attention consideration should be given to keeping the look-out appraised of the current navigational situation with regard to expected traffic, buoyage, weather, landfall, pilotage and any other circumstance relevant to good watchkeeping.*

## 10.0 *In Restricted Visibility*

10.1 *When restricted visibility is encountered or expected, the first responsibility of the OOW is to comply with the ColRegs with particular regard to the keeping of a look-out, sounding of fog signals, proceeding at a safe speed and having the engines ready for immediate manoeuvre.*

10.2 *In addition the OOW shall:*

- *Inform the Master*
- *ensure that a dedicated look-out is posted at all times*
- *exhibit navigation lights*
- *operate and use the radar*
- *put the engines on standby.*

## 11.0 *Safe Speed and Stopping Distance*

11.1 *The ColRegs require that every vessel shall at all times proceed at a safe speed so that proper effective action can be taken to avoid collision and be stopped within a distance appropriate to the prevailing circumstances and conditions.*

11.2 *In cases of need, the OOW shall not hesitate to use the engines to reduce speed further and allow more time for consideration and assessment of a developing situation. However, timely notice of the intended variations of engine speed shall be given to the engineers where possible or effective use made of UMS engine controls.*

11.3 *Whatever the pressure on Masters to make a quick passage or to meet the wishes of owners, operators, charterers or port operators, it does not justify vessels and those on board them being unnecessarily put at risk. The MCA is concerned that proper standards be maintained and will take appropriate action against officers who jeopardize their vessels or the lives and property of others. Such action may lead to fines and/or the suspension or cancellation of their certificates.*

11.4 *In the well known case of THE LADY GWENDOLEN, the Court of Appeal stated that "excessive speed in fog is a grave breach of duty and vessel owners should use their influence to prevent it." Because of their failure to do so, it was held in that case that the owners could not limit their liability.*

12.0 *Vessel at Anchor*

12.1 *The OOW shall:*

- *Determine and plot the vessel's position on the appropriate chart as soon as practicable*
- *when circumstances permit, check at sufficiently frequent intervals whether the vessel is remaining securely at anchor by taking bearings of fixed navigation marks or readily identifiable shore objects. The use of carefully chosen transits can give an almost instant indication as to whether the vessel's position has changed*
- *ensure that a proper look-out is maintained*
- *ensure that inspection rounds are made periodically*
- *observe meteorological and tidal conditions and state of sea, notify the Master and undertake all necessary measures if the vessel drags anchor*
- *ensure the state of readiness of the main engines and other machinery complies with the Master's requirements*
- *ensure the vessel exhibits the appropriate lights and shapes and that appropriate ColRegs sound signals are made*
- *avoid placing reliance on guard zones when using radar in lieu of a look-out as this is not considered acceptable practice.*

*In all the above circumstances it remains the Master's responsibility to ensure that the anchor watch to be kept is appropriate to the prevailing conditions.*

**13.0** *Certification*

13.1 *The Regulations require that any officer in charge of a navigational watch shall be duly qualified in accordance with the requirements of STCW 95. It is the responsibility of the owner or operator, and Master to ensure that every navigational watchkeeping officer is appropriately qualified with respect to the size of the vessel and limitations in area of operation. Under no circumstances is it permitted for an unqualified person to take charge of a navigational watch.*

13.2 *Similarly STCW 95 Section A-II/4 requires that every rating forming part of a navigational watch on a seagoing vessel of 500gt or more shall be required to demonstrate competence in the duties associated with the keeping of a safe navigational watch at the support level. This competence is evidenced by the issue of a Navigational Watch Rating Certificate. No rating should be assigned to navigational watchkeeping duties unless suitably qualified.*

13.3 *A qualification demonstrates that the holder has reached a minimum level of competence as defined in STCW 95. However, it does not imply that the holder has achieved all the necessary management or operational experience particular to a vessel, its operation or operational area. In considering an officer's or rating's qualifications due consideration should also be given to an individual's experience with respect to the vessel type and/or area of operation(s). In some circumstances it may be prudent to 'double-up' a watch or provide additional supervision to a qualified watchkeeper whilst particular operational experience is achieved.*

## 4.9    Other Considerations

### 4.9.1    Unsafe port – unsafe berth

You should be attentive to the possibility that a port or berth may become unsafe during your stay or visit. If you are concerned that your vessel may become damaged, eg due to prevailing weather conditions or the condition of the berth, you should take appropriate action immediately.

Before approaching any berth or terminal where you have any suspicion that there could be a problem with the berth, you should consider taking a number of photographs before berthing as evidence of the condition of the berth.

### 4.9.2    Sailing on a critical RPM for a prolonged period of time

Should you be instructed or required to proceed over a period of time within the critical RPM range, you should notify the engine room to prevent any damage to the vessel's propulsion system.

### 4.9.3    Sufficient tug assistance

The main cause of damage to locks, berths and the vessel herself is insufficient tug assistance, particularly in areas of prevailing strong tides and/or winds.

Proper consideration should be given to the level of tug assistance required to enable your vessel to arrive and depart safely from a port or berth.

A standard towage contract will allocate any liability to the vessel being towed even if there is no fault or negligence on their part.

It is generally difficult to prove any fault or negligence on the part of the tug as most towage contracts are based on the fact that the tug is the servant of the tow, even where the navigation is conducted by the tug.

Any damage claims by the tug are often lodged after completion of the work. Therefore, your owners and ultimately your P&I Club may be held liable when a tug is damaged or causes any damage during any berthing or unberthing operation.

Any damage to your own vessel will affect your hull and machinery insurance cover, as the tug's liability is generally excluded under most towage contracts.

When working with tugs, you should:

- Be alert when any manoeuvres are carried out by your own vessel or the tug(s)
- always be aware as to the position of any tugs
- always monitor your own vessel's speed to avoid overrunning the tug
- co-operate with the pilot and tug master.

Tugs' names and the time the tugs were made fast/released should be recorded in the bridge movement book.

### 4.9.4   Parametric/synchronous rolling

It is important to continually monitor any changes in the vessel's trim and/or rolling period to avoid excessive rolling (referred to as parametric or synchronous rolling). A ship can quickly generate large angles of roll together with violent pitch and yaw motions when the following conditions occur:

- The vessel is in head or near head seas (head on seas result in lower ship's speed, which results in larger roll motions)
- the length of the waves, crest to crest, is of a similar length to your own vessel
- the height of the waves is greater than the height which allows the natural pitch/roll cycle of the vessel to harmonise with the period of oncoming waves).

# 5 Cargo

The cargo is the responsibility of the Chief Officer. Any good Chief Officer will wish to deal directly with it and only come to you for advice, which is to be encouraged. However, while he is responsible for the cargo, he is also responsible to you, and you in turn are responsible to the company.

The Chief Officer must know how you wish to work with him and the areas where you wish to be kept informed or consulted. Provided you are in agreement with his actions, he must also know that he can rely on your full support in any dealings with the port authorities.

Responsible Officer: Master
Action Officer: Chief Officer designated Cargo Officer

## 5.1    Responsibilities

The Chief Officer is responsible for

- The planning and loading of all cargo
- preparing the cargo handling equipment
- the safe stability of the vessel at all times
- monitoring the cargo onboard
- the efficient cargo watch in port.

## 5.2    Voyage Orders

The Chief Officer must ascertain:

### 5.2.1   Dry cargo carriers

- ☑ The voyage number
- ☑ the ETA at load or discharge port
- ☑ draught at load or discharge port
- ☑ the name of the terminal
- ☑ the quantity and type of cargo to load/discharge
- ☑ laydays
- ☑ the ship's speed en route - maximum, chartered speed or economic
- ☑ safe port/safe berth
- ☑ name and communications addresses of agents
- ☑ communications schedules
- ☑ notices of ETA
- ☑ any pertinent charter party clauses
- ☑ bunkering port.

### Special requirements

- ☑ Any stowage requirements
- ☑ any special hold preparation requirements
- ☑ hold and cargo surveys
- ☑ instructions for cargo work in rain
- ☑ ventilation requirements
- ☑ routeing requirements.

### Prior to arrival, from the agent

- ☑ Confirmation of receipt of ETA
- ☑ confirmation of pilot ordered or anchor instructions
- ☑ which side alongside
- ☑ number of loaders or discharge grabs
- ☑ loading rate
- ☑ berth number, length and draught
- ☑ ship or shore gangway

- ☑ confirmation of acceptance of load or discharge plan
- ☑ port forms required and number of copies
- ☑ bunkers/stores/fresh water advice
- ☑ time of attendance and granting of port clearance.

## On arrival

- ☑ Confirmation of receipt and acceptance of notice of readiness (NOR).

## 5.2.2 Tankers

- ☑ The voyage number
- ☑ the ETA at the load port(s)
- ☑ terminal name
- ☑ loading date range
- ☑ quantity and grade of cargo(es) to load
- ☑ identification of cargo inspector
- ☑ cargo sampling instructions
- ☑ port clearance information
- ☑ cargo supplier
- ☑ consignor
- ☑ B/L number
- ☑ the ship's speed en route and/or required ETA at discharge port
- ☑ cargo instructions, including:
  - cargo tank preparations for the next cargo
  - any cargo heating requirements
  - cargo and vapour segregation requirements
  - vapour recovery (where applicable)
  - load-on-top instructions
  - any other relevant information (ship/consignor's agent, etc)

☑    information about the discharge port, which may include:
- port name
- terminal/berth
- discharge date
- identification of cargo inspector
- cargo sampling instructions
- port clearance information
- consignee
- cargo instructions, including:
  - vapour balance
  - discharge temperature
  - any other relevant information (ship/receiver's agent, etc).

## 5.3   Cargo Records

### 5.3.1   Oil tankers

The following papers must be retained for each cargo:

- ☑ Cargo nomination email (or telex)
- ☑ NOR
- ☑ cargo plan
- ☑ ship/shore safety checklist
- ☑ cargo log sheet (including pumping log)
- ☑ certificate of discharge
- ☑ also, where issued:
    - receipt for any ballast/slops discharged
    - letter(s) of protest
    - request for water plug
    - B/L.

### 5.3.2   Bulk and general cargo ships

- ☑ Cargo orders
- ☑ stowage plan
- ☑ discharge plan
- ☑ ballast replacement plan
- ☑ ballast discharge and load plan
- ☑ all communications regarding cargo, including copies of emails
- ☑ NOR
- ☑ notes of protest
- ☑ letters of protest
- ☑ hold survey certificates
- ☑ cargo chemical analysis and hazard data sheets
- ☑ any dangerous goods declarations
- ☑ moisture content certificate
- ☑ draught surveys - initial, intermediate and final
- ☑ cargo survey certificate
- ☑ rain indemnity
- ☑ Master's receipts
- ☑ arrival draught calculations
- ☑ discharge programme

- ☑ damage report
- ☑ timesheets
- ☑ off-hire report
- ☑ cargo log.

## 5.3.3   The cargo log

- ☑ How you want the cargo stowed or loaded
- ☑ lashing and dunnaging if a dry cargo
- ☑ the cargo plan
- ☑ recording of damage to cargo
- ☑ the ballasting programme
- ☑ topping off of tanks
- ☑ soundings
- ☑ overboard discharge
- ☑ stoppages
- ☑ when to be called
- ☑ handover
- ☑ cargo disputes.

## 5.4    Cargo Loading

☑  Prior to loading a cargo, the Chief Officer must ensure that the ship is ready to receive it

☑  he should prepare an initial loading plan based on the charterer's requirements. This plan must then be sent to the charterer

☑  once the plan is accepted and the cargo is confirmed, a detailed loading plan must be prepared and sent to the load port

☑  throughout these operations, the Master should be consulted about the stresses, draught and trim

☑  the Chief Officer must ensure that, prior to arrival, all Deck Officers are fully conversant with the cargo loading plan

☑  he must ensure that all local port regulations are complied with

☑  the ship/shore safety checklist or port compliance form should be given to the terminal for signature

☑  the Chief Officer must complete the deadweight report

☑  on completion, the Chief Officer must ensure that the ship is secured and make a log book entry to that effect.

## 5.5   Discharge

- ☑ The Chief Officer must make a discharge plan and forward this to the agents at the discharge port
- ☑ he must ensure all deck officers are fully conversant with the plan
- ☑ on completion, he must ensure that the ship is ballasted and ready for sea
- ☑ he should ensure that the ship is secured and make a log entry to this effect.

## 5.6    Cargo Checklists – Oil Tankers

### 5.6.1    Arrival at a terminal using a Vapour Emission Control System (VECS)

Before arriving at a loading port where a VECS is used, it is essential that the following preparations are carried out:

☑ Contact the terminal to determine:
- diameter of the vapour line to be used (so the appropriate vapour line reducer can be fitted)
- maximum liquid transfer rate
- requirements for additional processing (purging) of vapour in cargo oil tanks (the facility may impose limits on oxygen, hydrocarbon and hydrogen sulphide content)

☑ purge the tanks to reduce the oxygen content to less than 8% by volume and the hydrogen sulphide content to 10 ppm or less

☑ check the operation of the fixed closed tank gauging system

☑ check the operation of the portable closed gauging system

☑ set high level alarms to no greater than 95% of the tank volume and test the visible and audible alarms

☑ test overfill alarms for each tank

☑ isolate the inert gas system from the deck main

☑ check function and pressure settings of each tank P/V valve or high velocity vent

☑ check the function and setting of any P/V relief valve on the inert gas distribution pipeline

☑ check that the liquid level in the deck seal is correct

☑ ensure that the cargo transfer plan is consistent with the VECS manual required under the IMO Standards for Vapour Emission Control Systems, MSC/Circ.585 and MARPOL Annex VI, Regulation 15 and USCG 46 CFR 39, as appropriate

☑ briefly open the drain line to clear the system of any condensate

☑ check the electrical conductivity, ensuring that the vapour piping is correctly grounded to the hull with a maximum resistance of no more than 10 KΩ

☑   check the function and settings of the audible and visual high and low pressure alarms for the inert gas distribution piping system
☑   check the integrity of the manifold valve
☑   reduce the tank pressure to 10 mb (100 mmWG or 1 kPa).

## 5.6.2   Cargo valve failure

If the cargo valve control system fails during cargo operations, the following actions should be carried out:

☑   If the cargo valve hydraulic system leaks, sections of the pipeline system should be isolated, ensuring that the maximum number of valves can be hydraulically operated. It is helpful to have an isolation plan, posted in the cargo control room, so that valves that can be operated when sections of the hydraulic pipeline are isolated
☑   arrange for crew members to be available to operate valves manually
☑   place portable units in positions where they will be most effective and require minimum effort to move
☑   valves with an auto/manual change-over set up should be switched to manual operation. A prominent notice should be posted at the valve control position, making it clear which valves have been switched to manual control
☑   regularly check on critical isolation valves that cannot be manually operated, ensuring they remain closed
☑   arrangements should be made to ensure that critical isolation valves that have been switched to manual control are not inadvertently opened
☑   when loading cargo, the transfer rate should be reassessed because of the extra time required to operate valves manually
☑   personnel involved in the operation should be briefed and given familiarisation training in the use of portable hydraulic units.

## 5.6.3   Failure of Inert Gas System (IGS)

When a serious failure of the IGS occurs during cargo operations, the following should be carried out:

☑ Stop cargo operations and close all valves

☑ advise the port authority, if necessary

☑ make the necessary notifications required by the operator's procedures

☑ advise the facility representative

☑ check for any leaks on the venting system and confirm that the cargo openings are tightly closed. Any leaks found must be managed without opening cargo oil tanks

☑ institute control measures to prevent the opening of any tank vents, valves or tank openings

☑ monitor tank pressures if possible

☑ prepare for the possibility of continuing operations with an external inert gas supply.

### 5.6.4 Oil discharge monitoring equipment (ODME) failure

When an ODME failure occurs and discharge control can only be carried out manually, overboard discharge must be stopped and an entry made in the Oil Record Book Part II, Cargo/Ballast Operations (Oil Tankers), operational code M, alongside items 70, 71 and 72. The recorded times of when the system failed, was repaired and made operational should be consistent with the ODME printouts. The record of the failure should be factual and supported by a technician's report.

If the unit cannot be repaired onboard, the tanker's operator must be advised and arrangements made for a technician to attend or for the spare parts to be delivered at the next port of call.

MARPOL Annex 1 Regulation 31, Oil discharge monitoring and control system, states that:

*"A failure of the monitoring and control system shall stop the discharge. In the event of failure of the oil discharge monitoring and control system a manually operated alternative method may be used. The defective unit must be made operable as soon as possible. With the permission of the flag state authority, a tanker with a defective oil discharge monitoring and control system may undertake one ballast voyage before proceeding to a repair port."*

If a failure occurs during the ballast passage, ballast or slops from cargo oil tanks can be discharged under permitted conditions with the ODME operated in manual mode. The following must be carried out:

- ☑ The Master's authorisation should be sought before operating the ODME in manual mode
- ☑ the tanker operator's procedure for manual operation of ODME should be implemented
- ☑ the manufacturer's approved instructions for manual operation must be followed strictly
- ☑ when monitoring the effluent discharge can only be carried out visually, it must be carried out during daylight hours only
- ☑ during discharge, the oil/water interface must be continually checked using an approved oil/water interface detector
- ☑ when dirty ballast is discharged, a small amount should be left in each tank being deballasted. This should be transferred to a designated slop tank for decanting.

If the ODME is unable to provide data automatically, the following methods can be used to determine the required information:

- ■ If the oil content cannot be determined automatically due to the oil content or sampling system failing, it can be estimated using a visual observation of the sea surface in the area of the overboard discharge, in combination with the oil/water interface level measurements taken from tanks that are being deballasted
- ■ if the flow meter fails, the flow rate can be approximated by referring to the pump characteristic curve under the actual discharge conditions, or it can be determined by the calculation of changes in ballast volume using cargo oil tank calibration tables
- ■ when a failure renders speed indication unavailable, speed can be calculated using rpm, propeller diameter, pitch and predicted slip
- ■ when failure renders geographical position information unavailable, a position can be obtained from other position fixing instruments onboard.

If a processor fails, the instantaneous rate of discharge and total oil content can be calculated using the following formulae:

$$\text{Instantaneous rate of discharge} = \frac{\text{estimated oil content (ppm)} \times \text{flow rate (m}^3\text{/h)}}{1000 \times \text{speed (knots)}} \text{ l/nm}$$

$$\text{Oil discharged} = \frac{\text{flow rate (m}^3\text{/h)} \times \text{oil content (ppm)} \times \text{time (mins)*}}{60,000} \text{ litres}$$

*The oil discharged in the second equation refers to the time interval in minutes, when the oil content of the effluent is considered to be constant.

The total oil discharged, which must be no greater than 1/30,000 of the volume of the previous cargo, is the aggregate or running total of the oil discharged calculations.

For example, a tanker travelling at 15 knots, discharging dirty ballast with an oil content of 60 ppm at 1,000 m³/h for 8 minutes, then ballast with an oil content of 80 ppm at 900 m³/h for 6 minutes:

$$\text{The instantaneous rate of discharge is constant} = \frac{60 \times 1,000}{1,000 \times 15} = 4 \text{ litres/nm}$$

$$\text{The oil discharged} = \frac{1,000 \times 60 \times 8}{60,000} = 8 \text{ litres}$$

$$\text{The instantaneous rate of discharge is constant} = \frac{80 \times 900}{1,000 \times 15} = \frac{72,000}{15,000}$$
$$= 4.8 \text{ litres/nm}$$

$$\text{The oil discharged} = \frac{900 \times 80 \times 6}{60,000} = \frac{72,000}{10,000} = 7.2 \text{ litres}$$

Total oil discharged = 8 + 7.2 = 15.2 litres

Pump speed and discharge valve operation should be controlled manually, ensuring that the flow rate of the discharge overboard is such that the instantaneous rate of discharge of oil does not exceed 30 litres per nautical mile.

## 5.7    Signing Bills of Lading (B/L) - Letters of Indemnity

The difficulties and liabilities arising from issuing and signing B/Ls is an area that your P&I Club should have published guidance on. The information contained here is for rapid reference only.

### General

A bill of lading is a valuable legal document with three very important functions:

- It is a document of title
- it is evidence of the contract of carriage between the company and the cargo interests
- it is a receipt for the goods loaded.

When signing the B/L, it is important that you ensure the information is accurate. If it is inaccurate or false, there will be serious consequences for your company or charterer, including exposure to possible claims from other cargo interests. This is particularly the case if the B/L has been endorsed to a third party consignee.

If the B/L is traded while the vessel is en route to the discharge port, an innocent buyer will not be aware of the actual condition or quantity of the cargo. The details in the B/L are therefore considered to be conclusive evidence of the condition and quantity of the goods when shipped. The company will be unable to defend any claim if the actual condition or quantity of the cargo is not in accordance with that stated in the B/L.

Your P&I cover may be affected as P&I rules tend to exclude cover for claims in certain circumstances where the information in the B/L is found to be incorrect.

Particular attention should be paid to the following details:

- Description of the condition and quantity of the cargo
- date of issue of the B/L.

If the cargo is seriously damaged, or you are unsure as to the extent of the damage, especially in the case of steel cargoes, the Master should contact the P&I correspondent to arrange for a survey.

If there appears to be no damage to the cargo, you should write on the B/L that the cargo was received 'in apparent good order and condition'.

The B/L must also record the correct quantity of cargo loaded. If not, the B/L should be claused 'weight and quantity unknown' or 'said to weigh'. You should note on the face of the B/L if the vessel's figures differ from the shore figures.

## Date of issue

A 'shipped on board' B/L confirms that the cargo was loaded onto the vessel on a particular date. The date of shipment often has important implications, eg in the contract of sale between the shipper and receiver. If the date is incorrect, the company or charterer may face claims from the receiver. The B/L must therefore be signed and dated to record accurately the date when the cargo was actually loaded. You must not sign a post-dated B/L.

## Authority on behalf of the Master to sign B/L

When charterers or agents are authorised to sign the B/L on your behalf, you should ensure that all the details you would have inserted into the B/L with regard to quantity, condition and date are inserted into the Mate's receipt. You should ensure that the charterers and/or agents are instructed to sign the B/L only in accordance with the Mate's receipt. If charterers and/or agents refuse to do so, you must issue a letter of protest and inform the company immediately. Your P&I correspondent may also be able to assist.

Letters of indemnity

It is common practice for the shipper to offer a letter of indemnity in exchange for a clean B/L or a B/L that is postdated. Such letters of indemnity are unenforceable in most jurisdictions because the courts consider the carrier a party, with the shippers, to a fraud, ie the B/L is issued in the knowledge that it contains information on which the receivers will rely, but which is known to be incorrect.

A letter of indemnity is therefore not legally binding and will offer the company no protection if the shipper goes back on his promise. There will be no P&I cover available either as the P&I rules exclude cover for claims arising from the issue of a postdated B/L or claims arising from the issue of a B/L known to contain an incorrect description of cargo, its quantity or condition.

Whenever you are requested to issue a clean or incorrectly dated B/L in return for a letter of indemnity, you should:

- Refuse, despite threats to delay the vessel or other pressures
- immediately contact the company and/or the P&I correspondent for advice and assistance.

# 6 Meetings

Meetings are important and useful, such as planning meetings for port arrival, dry-docking, safety, cargo planning or repairs. Although most meetings onboard tend to be informal, the following are some useful guidelines for planning and conducting the activity. These considerations apply equally to ships with large crew numbers with various specialised departments and to smaller crews, particularly for weekly management and regular safety committee meetings.

Responsible Officer: Master

## 6.1 Safety Committee Meetings

The Code of Safe Working Practice for Merchant Seamen recommends that safety committee meetings occur at intervals of 4-6 weeks, although it recognises the need for flexibility. It is very prescriptive in format, structure and who should attend, ie at least the Master, Safety Officer and Safety Representatives.

It states that the Master should act as Chairman, and it is improbable, in all but departmental meetings, that any other member of the crew would take this role.

## 6.2    General Guidelines

All meetings must have a clear objective, which should be advised to all participants in advance or at the start of the meeting.

The Chairman plays an important role in controlling the meeting and steering it towards its intended objective. If appropriate, meetings can be structured with an agenda and, wherever possible, this should be circulated well in advance of the meeting.

The first duty of the Chairman is to start the meeting on time, welcoming the participants, stating the objective(s) and reviewing the previous minutes. This establishes the Chairman's authority, sets the appropriate level of formality, and focuses the group mind.

The Chairman should not:

- Use the position to demonstrate his knowledge
- allow familiarity to obscure the importance of the meeting
- give too much direction or introduction to each item
- become too involved in debate
- make cynical, oppressive or demeaning retorts
- interfere with the outcome of the final decision.

An effective Chairman will:

- Remain calm, alert and attentive
- make swift and equitable decisions
- maintain good order
- remain impartial but take action when necessary
- encourage and ensure all participants have the opportunity to speak
- limit the number of interruptions in the meeting by protecting the person speaking
- act as facilitator, managing the meeting
- ensure progress is made in line with the items on the agenda
- keep discussions to the point and prevent unrelated subjects taking over
- not interfere with the direction or final decisions.

It may sometimes be appropriate for the Chief Engineer or Chief Officer to take the lead in discussions, for example on technical matters, and this can enable the Master to gain a better understanding of the matter under discussion. By taking a step back, he can also observe the personalities and dynamics of the crew.

For formal meetings (such as Safety Committee meetings) minutes should be taken and circulated as soon as possible after the meeting to maintain momentum. The minutes should record concisely the matters discussed, decisions reached, further actions to be taken and the identity of the person(s) responsible for undertaking each action.

It is the Chairman's duty to formally close the meeting, and closing remarks should be kept brief and positive. He must not allow the meeting just to peter out because part of the group believes it is over as this can detract from the perceived importance of the meeting.

At the end of each meeting, an appropriate date for the next meeting should be set.

# 7 Communications

When they took away radio officers they didn't take away the work, and there was little regard made for the fact that a radio officer didn't spend all his time onboard tapping his morse key. The work remains and now has to be undertaken by someone else.

Responsible Officer: 2nd Officer

Responsibilities

- Maintenance of all communication equipment
- maintenance of all electronic bridge equipment
- instruction of the ship's company in safety communications
- requisition and maintenance of all spares and stores required
- correction of the Admiralty Lists of Radio Signals (ALRS)
- preparation of all radio and telephone accounts
- requisition and maintenance of all ship's stationery requirements
- requisition and maintenance of all flags
- maintenance of the GMDSS Log Book.

## 7.1  Repairs and Surveys

- ☑ When any fault is found with the ship's communication system (GMDSS) or with any electronic bridge equipment, a repair chit should be made out to the officer responsible for communications
- ☑ he will look at the equipment and advise the head of department of any repair that is required
- ☑ should shore technical assistance be required, the company should be advised
- ☑ the 2nd Officer is responsible for signing the work sheet and completion papers for the attendance of any shore technician
- ☑ he is also responsible for safety radio surveys and attending to the surveyor.

## 7.2    Administration

A number of the administrative functions will be carried out by the Master, but certain items can be delegated to others onboard. Delegation is not always easy but if you do not do so your officers will not have the opportunity to learn what is required of them, even if that means learning from mistakes.

As more and more administrative functions continue to be expected of the ship, and key officers of the past such as the Purser, the Chief Steward and the Radio Officer are removed, the modern Master must make best use of the abilities of his officers. A considerable amount of the ship's administration will be carried out by the Master, but there is no reason why another officer cannot be appointed as the ship's administration officer to assist.

For this section, assume such an appointment has been made. What follows is a suggested job specification for the appointment.

Responsible Officer: Master

Action Officer: As designated

### 7.2.1   Responsibilities

- ☑ Preparation of the monthly food stock accounts
- ☑ control of the ship's administration office
- ☑ reception of port officials and visitors
- ☑ preparation of port papers, including:
  - customs declaration
  - stores lists
  - crew lists
  - port health
  - list of narcotics
  - list of arms and ammunition
  - passenger declaration
  - emergency contact list
- ☑ issue of, and accounting, for the bond
- ☑ preparation and issue of cash advances

☑   advance weekly cash requirements
☑   the ship's postal services
☑   preparation of the company mail envelopes and listing of contents
☑   care of the official documents and personnel files of the officers and crew
☑   filing and correction of all the company fleet instructions.

## 7.2.2   Administrative functions

☑   Administrative matters of the ship may be dealt with by the administration officer designated by the Master
☑   all personnel with questions on pay or the ship's administration should, in the first instance, refer their questions directly to the administration officer
☑   prior to arrival in port, the administration officer should prepare the port entry papers as detailed in the 'Guide to Port Entry'
☑   on arrival in port, he should receive the port officials on the gangway and conduct them to the port reception room and, in the absence of the Master, begin the ship's clearance
☑   in the absence of the Master, he should deal with the agent on ship matters
☑   he should receive all visitors to the ship in the port reception room and arrange the attendance of relevant ship's personnel when required
☑   on departure, he should collect mail from the ship's mail box and give this, together with the official mail, to the agent.

# 8 Accommodation

## 8.1 Hotel Services

On many ships, a Chief Steward is not carried and the Chief Cook carries out the duties of Chief Steward. Often he does not have the experience required to assume the traditional duties of the catering department and, in this case, certain procedures are suggested to assist him in the interests of the efficiency of this department.

Do consider the needs of this department, which is expected to work seven days a week, continually judged and to continue with the same work regardless of weather or conditions onboard.

It is important to ensure that the crew is responsible for their part of the ship and that the same standard of cleanliness is maintained in all areas.

Regardless of the size of ship, the weekly inspection should be a formal occasion with effort made to prepare the ship for it. It is an occasion for praise and reprimand, and for noting deficiencies that should be dealt with before the next inspection.

Responsible Officer: Master

Action Officer: Chief Officer, Chief Steward or Chief Cook

## 8.2    Working Hours and Overtime

- Working hours and overtime records are the responsibility of the Chief Steward or Chief Cook
- at the end of the month, he should submit the overtime figures of the catering department to the Chief Officer.

## 8.3   Cleanliness

The officers' quarters are serviced as follows:

Steward 1 is responsible for:

- ☑ Service in the officers' saloon
- ☑ cleanliness of the officers' pantry, duty mess, saloon and smoke room
- ☑ cleanliness and maintenance of all officers' cutlery and crockery
- ☑ cleanliness of the hospital (and passenger cabins if any)
- ☑ cleanliness of the accommodation deck, alleyways, stairs and bulkheads
- ☑ distribution of laundry, bath soap and cleaning materials to the crew
- ☑ cleaning officers' cabins as designated
- ☑ officers' laundry.

Steward 2 is responsible for:

- ☑ Serving officers' lunch in the duty mess
- ☑ assisting with the washing and maintenance of the officers' cutlery and crockery
- ☑ cleanliness of the accommodation deck passages, stairs and bulkheads
- ☑ cleanliness of designated officers' cabins
- ☑ assisting the Chief Cook in cleaning and general duties
- ☑ assisting Steward 1
- ☑ officers' laundry.

### 8.3.1   Ratings' quarters

- ☑ Ratings' cabins are cleaned by the occupants
- ☑ ratings' quarters and public areas are cleaned by all departmental ratings, as designated by the Bosun.

## 8.3.2   Inspections

☑    All the accommodation should be inspected every week by the Master and heads of department

☑    the Bosun should accompany the inspection party for all crew areas

☑    all food storage rooms and refrigeration chambers must be inspected

☑    the Chief Officer should make a note of all defects and report them to the various departments for action

☑    all cabins should be vacated for inspection unless special exemption has been granted. Normal watchkeeping is not exempted

☑    keep a keen eye for any suspicious articles or strange conditions onboard.

Accommodation inspections have to go beyond just checking everything is 'present and correct' and in a clean condition. They should in particular look for deficiencies in any of the following areas:

☑    Spare gear lockers
☑    cabins
☑    messrooms
☑    galley
☑    storerooms
☑    refrigeration spaces
☑    toilets.

Many things can be wrong with the ship but if the food is good, the galley clean and the catering well managed, much will be forgiven. Get these wrong and problems will surely follow.

If you have no Chief Steward, you must ensure that the crew are consulted in decisions regarding their food.

Bedding is the most neglected area on most ships. Bedding should be clean and, if the cleaning cannot be done by the ship's laundry, send it ashore. If the condition of mattresses is poor, new ones should be provided.

An unhygienic environment could lead to outbreaks of food poisoning onboard which can seriously affect the health of the crew and ultimately the safety of the ship. Clean and well kept galleys, storerooms and crew accommodation are the best means of ensuring the health of the crew.

Storerooms (including fridges and freezers) should be checked regularly and expiry dates for foodstuffs observed. Frozen food should be carefully checked for any signs of 'freezer burn' and any affected meat must be disposed of.

The entire water system needs to be regularly checked and cleaned. Careful maintenance of the entire water piping system, including the air conditioning unit, must take place at scheduled intervals to prevent the outbreak of bacterial infections such as Legionnaires' disease, especially when trading in areas with mild temperatures.

If fresh water is used in pools, regular water quality tests (bromine, hardness, PH, etc) must be carried out and recorded.

You should be aware that there are various ILO and Flag State regulations to be complied with and Port State Control may well inspect the accommodation, galleys and storerooms and take action if necessary.

## 8.4   Victualling

The following may be the procedure if a Chief Steward is not carried.

Responsible Officer: Master

Action Officers: Chief Cook

- ☑ The Chief Cook is responsible for the preparation of all the food
- ☑ the Chief Cook is responsible for the cleanliness and maintenance of all the galley, pantry and food store rooms
- ☑ the Chief Cook is responsible for menu preparation. He will prepare the menu book and present it to the Master each week
- ☑ the Chief Cook is responsible for the preparation of the list of food stores in good time before arrival at port
- ☑ a victualling committee is one approach to achieve balance of the stores onboard. This could consist of:
  - the Master
  - Deck Officer representative
  - Engineer Officer representative
  - deck crew representative
  - engine crew representative
- ☑ the victualling committee should meet before each order is submitted to the Chandler
- ☑ payment of bills should be authorised by the Master. The bills must be filed and available for inspection, clearly showing the rate of exchange and any discount allowed
- ☑ at the end of the month, the victualling accounts should be posted for the officers and crew
- ☑ any complaints regarding food, cooking or quality should initially be directed to the complainant's representative.

## 8.5   Laundry

- ☑ Ratings are responsible for the laundry of their own sheets, pillowcases and towels, apart from the clean items issued on joining
- ☑ officers' sheets, duvet covers, pillowcases and towels are changed for laundering every week
- ☑ dirty blankets or duvets are to be dry cleaned only, and should be sent ashore in selected ports.

## 8.6    Stores

Action Officer: Chief Cook

☑    Soap and soap powder must be issued to each cabin on the last day of the month

☑    the Chief Cook should keep a check of cabin stores and advise the Chief Officer of any requirements

☑    the Chief Cook should make a list of required items for the 6 months' requisition and hand this to the Chief Officer.

# 9 Personnel

New personnel joining a ship have a right to enter clean cabins, to find that their essential stores and safety equipment are provided and in order, and to be received correctly. The reception of those at sea for the first time is exceptionally important as their first impressions may affect their attitude onboard.

Responsible Officer: Master

## 9.1 Joining Procedure

Action Officers: Chief Officer, 1st Engineer Officer and Chief Steward/ Chief Cook

- ☑ Prior to personnel joining, the cabin they are to occupy must be cleaned
- ☑ the Chief Steward/Chief Cook must ensure that fresh linen, towels and blankets are issued for all newly joined personnel
- ☑ the Chief Steward/Chief Cook must ensure that joining information and checklists are placed in the cabins of new arrivals
- ☑ on their arrival, newly joined personnel should be accompanied by their superior to the Master's Office to hand over their documents and pay forms. They will then sign the ship's articles of agreement
- ☑ the Bosun and Fitter must issue the required PPE and hand in the signed checklists to either the Chief Officer or the 1st Engineer Officer
- ☑ as soon as possible after joining, the Chief Officer and 1st Engineer Officer should arrange a guided tour of the ship. The Chief Officer is responsible for the catering department personnel
- ☑ it is important that heads of department meet their new personnel as soon as possible, and check that the joining procedure has been followed
- ☑ in the case of large crew changes, a general emergency drill and boat stations muster should be held as soon as possible after sailing.

## 9.2    New Joiner Induction

These are to meet the requirements of the Safety Management System, STCW 95 and ISM Code.

### 9.2.1    Deck officers

These items are to be completed by all deck officers joining. As many of the following items should be completed during the handover period and as much time as possible made available to the joining and leaving officers.

If insufficient time is available for the handover, the Chief Officer will be responsible for completing the familiarisation of the equipment and procedures concerning the deck department.

- ☑ Bridge equipment, including:
    - voyage plan
    - autopilot/steering console
    - electronic navigation aids
    - GMDSS
    - electronic charts
    - ARPA/RADAR/ECDIS
    - deck stress monitoring system
    - location of manuals
- ☑ alarms:
    - general emergency
    - lifeboat stations
    - $CO_2$ release
- ☑ main engine controls:
    - bridge
    - emergency steering gear
- ☑ IGS
- ☑ cargo system:
    - cargo pumproom (including entry procedures)
- ☑ Crude Oil Washing (COW) system
- ☑ mooring patterns:
    - mooring winch controls
    - anchoring procedures

- ☑ safety induction of the vessel to include:
  - muster stations – lifeboat and emergency
  - fixed fire-fighting equipment (FFE)
  - $CO_2$ smothering
  - portable FFE
  - lifesaving equipment
  - emergency escape routes
  - remote stops and trips
  - PPE
- ☑ briefing prior to taking up duties on:
  - man overboard
  - casualty in enclosed space
  - closing of fire and watertight doors
  - explanation of safety symbols
- ☑ current security level/CSO and SSO designations:
  - where security information is detailed
  - gangway/visitors log/pass system and procedures
  - basic lockdown and sealing procedures, as required
  - restricted areas/procedures
- ☑ Master's standing orders read and understood
- ☑ company standing orders
- ☑ handover notes read and understood (copy placed in ISM office file).

## 9.2.2  Catering

These items are to be completed by all crew joining. As many of the following items should be completed during the handover period and as much time as possible made available to the joining and leaving crew.

If insufficient time is available for the handover, the Master will be responsible for completing the familiarisation of the equipment and procedures concerning the catering department.

- ☑ Alarms:
  - general emergency
  - lifeboat stations
  - fridge

- ☑ garbage management procedure
- ☑ safe operation of food processing equipment including cleaning instructions
- ☑ operation of water boilers, kettles and toasters
- ☑ hygiene standards
- ☑ accommodation cleaning routine
- ☑ general cleaning routines
- ☑ dress codes
- ☑ food handling procedures
- ☑ management of the fridges/dry stores, including stock control and storing procedures
- ☑ operation and safety of any high voltage equipment in the galley, including the main range and baker's ovens
- ☑ breakfast/lunch/dinner procedures
- ☑ safety induction of the vessel to include:
  - muster stations – lifeboat and emergency
  - fixed fire-fighting equipment (FFE)
  - $CO_2$ smothering
  - portable FFE
  - lifesaving equipment
  - emergency escape routes
  - remote stops and trips
  - PPE
- ☑ briefing prior to taking up duties on:
  - man overboard
  - casualty in enclosed space
  - closing of fire and watertight doors
  - explanation of safety symbols
- ☑ current security level/CSO and SSO designations:
  - where security information is detailed
  - gangway/visitors log/pass system and procedures
  - basic lockdown and sealing procedures as required
  - restricted areas/procedures
- ☑ company standing orders.

## 9.3    Crew Qualifications and Documentation

### 9.3.1   Crew qualifications

For all new crew that are assigned to the vessel, you should ensure that they are qualified and certificated appropriately for the voyage and that they meet the requirements of:

- ☑ The vessel's Flag State
- ☑ STCW 95.

### 9.3.2   Crew documentation

Crew documentation includes:

- Certificates of competency
- Flag State certification and endorsements
- correct seafarer's identification book
- vaccination certificates
- training record book
- medical certificate.

### 9.3.3   Crew competency

Each member of the crew should have the appropriate training and experience to perform their allocated duties. For newly joined crew members, you should satisfy yourself that they:

- Have a valid and genuine certificate of competency and the appropriate Flag State endorsements (eg dangerous cargo endorsement)
- are properly familiarised with their duties onboard, particularly those involved with watchkeeping duties
- are fit and healthy.

Any deficiency should be reported to the company and a replacement requested.

You can achieve a general impression of the qualifications of new crew members from their ISF Personal Training and Record Book, or any other similar documents, which should contain all the relevant information on their professional qualifications, training and service.

### 9.3.4   Crew fitness

You are required to monitor the fitness and health of your crew during the voyage, including:

- Alcohol consumption
- any signs of drug or medication abuse
- fatigue.

Should you observe any of the above, you should take appropriate corrective action without delay.

Particular attention should be paid to mandatory resting times prior to watches, as required by STCW 95, if applicable.

### 9.3.5 Crew fatigue

You should watch for any indications of fatigue or psychological unfitness and should, if necessary:

- Review working hours/workloads of the individuals concerned
- initiate a medical examination
- inform the company and request a substitution
- ensure ILO hours of work and rest requirements are adhered to and recorded correctly.

## 9.4    Leaving Procedure

Action Officers: Chief Officer, 1st Engineer Officer, Administration Officer and Chief Cook

- Prior to departure, all departing personnel must ensure that their cabins are clean
- ratings should hand all used linen and blankets to the Chief Cook. Stewards must replace the linen and blankets in the officers' cabins
- all personnel should hand in their ship issued PPE to the Bosun and Fitter and have their PPE checklist signed. This list is not to be signed without presentation of the cabin key
- leaving personnel must collect their documents and pay-off papers from the Master and, on presentation of the signed PPE checklist, sign off the ship's articles.

# 10 Discipline

At sea, we have to live and work in an environment that requires conformity. This requires rules that govern behaviour while on the ship.

Without discipline, no ship can properly function. Effective discipline coupled with a well managed ship that has a system in place for all grievances to be heard and addressed, provides the background for a pleasant and fair environment for all.

Discipline begins with the presentation and appearance of each crew member, and each should wear the correct safety clothing/PPE at all times. In port, each crew member should display an identification for officials and other visitors to see.

Discipline is best achieved out of respect. You must earn the respect of your officers and crew through the example of your leadership and management skills.

Responsible Officer: Master

Action Officers: All Officers and CPOs

## 10.1 Responsibilities

- Chief Petty Officers are the Bosun, who is the Senior Petty Officer and responsible for all the crew, the Fitter and the Chief Cook. They are immediately responsible for the ratings in their departments

- the Chief Officer is head of the deck department and the 1st Engineer Officer is in charge of personnel in the engine department. The Chief Officer, in the absence of a Chief Steward, is also head of the catering department for discipline and work matters
- the Chief Engineer is the head of the engine department
- the Master is head of the ship.

## 10.2 Ratings

- ☑ If any rating has a problem, relating either to his department or another aspect of shipboard management, he must first see his CPO
- ☑ if the CPO cannot deal satisfactorily with the problem, the CPO must advise the Chief Steward, Chief Officer or the 1st Engineer Officer of the situation
- ☑ the Chief Officer or 1st Engineer Officer should arrange a time to interview the rating concerned
- ☑ if the 1st Engineer Officer cannot resolve the problem, he should take the matter to the Chief Engineer
- ☑ if the Chief Engineer or Chief Officer cannot resolve the problem, they should refer the matter to the Master
- ☑ if the Master cannot resolve the problem to the rating's satisfaction, the matter should be referred to the company.

## 10.3 Officers

☑ Any complaint a CPO or junior officer may have regarding a rating or any other shipboard matter must go directly to the Chief Officer or 1st Engineer Officer

☑ should the 1st Engineer Officer be unable to resolve the matter, he should go to see the Chief Engineer

☑ if the Chief Officer or Chief Engineer cannot resolve the problem, the matter should be referred to the Master who will, if unable to resolve the problem, pass it to the company.

## 10.4 Disciplinary Procedure

☑ Any disciplinary proceedings that involve crew members must initially be dealt with by the Chief Officer or 1st Engineer Officer, in the presence of the rating's CPO. Should the 1st Engineer Officer consider that the case is serious, he should then take it before the Chief Engineer

☑ regardless of the way in which the situation is dealt with, the Master should be advised of the matter

☑ if the offence is of a serious nature and likely to involve officially recorded warnings or punishment, the case should be brought to the Master, who might then order a hearing

☑ a suitable time for a hearing will be arranged. The case will be heard in the presence of the Head of Department, CPO of the Department, the rating involved and any witnesses.

# 11 ISM and ISPS Codes

Compliance with the International Safety Management (ISM) Code is a critical necessity for modern shipping.

Responsible Officer: Master

Action Officers: Deck Department Safety Officer, Engine Department Safety Officer, Engine Department Accident Prevention Officer, Chief Steward/Chief Cook, Bosun and Fitter

## 11.1 Responsibilities

- Personnel involved in safety and environmental protection are responsible to the ship's Safety Officer
- CPOs are directly responsible for ensuring that those working under them are properly equipped for the work in hand
- the Safety Officer is responsible for ensuring that all safety equipment is in good order
- officers are responsible for ensuring that a safe environment exists within their department work areas
- the Safety Officer is responsible for ensuring that the correct equipment is available for the designated work
- department officers are responsible for ensuring that all PPE has been issued, is available and is used.

## 11.2  ISM Management

- ☑ The company SMS procedures must be adhered to and regularly reviewed
- ☑ any order given that involves any form of unsafe practice, puts a crew member in any form of danger or commits a crew member to work without the proper safety equipment is an illegal order
- ☑ CPOs must also ensure that the work is being carried out in a safe manner. If they feel that the work they are ordered to do is unsafe in any way or they do not have the correct equipment to do the work safely, they must immediately cease the work and request a review of the conditions or equipment by the officer ordering the work
- ☑ all departmental work must be recorded in a departmental work order book. Each item of work must be checked for conformity with ISM requirements. This notation must be signed by the officer giving the work order and the officer or crew member directly in charge of completing the work
- ☑ you must ensure that a common working language, understood by all onboard, is used
- ☑ all risk assessment requirements must be adhered to and followed.

## 11.3  ISPS Code Checklists

The International Code for the Security of Ships and of Port Facilities was adopted on the 12th of December 2002, and this now requires both port and ship to adopt security measures conforming to the level of security risk deemed to exist either by the ship or the port. There are three levels of security and each level requires the ship to be prepared to take certain actions as required. Such actions must be in accordance with the Ship Security Plan (SSP) and would include the following.

### 11.3.1 Ship's security level 1

- ☑ Check the identity and business of all persons wishing to board the ship
- ☑ in liaison with the port, establish designated secure areas for the searching of persons, personal effects, baggage, vehicles and their contents
- ☑ in liaison with the port, vehicles being loaded should be searched prior to loading with the frequency designated in the Ship's Security Plan
- ☑ all checked personnel and their personal effects are to be separated from unchecked persons and their effects
- ☑ embarking and disembarking passengers are to be segregated
- ☑ access points to be secured or guarded should be identified
- ☑ unattended spaces adjoining areas to which visitors or passengers have access should be secured
- ☑ brief all ship's company on the threat and the procedures for reporting suspicious persons, activities and objects.

### 11.3.2 Ship's security level 2

In addition to the above:

- ☑ Assign additional personnel to patrol deck areas during the silent hours
- ☑ limit the number of access points to the ship
- ☑ in liaison with the port, deter waterside access to the ship

☑ in liaison with the port, establish a restricted area on the shore side of the ship

☑ increase the frequency of searches of persons, effects and vehicles being embarked or loaded onto the ship

☑ escort visitors on the ship

☑ provide additional specific briefings on the security threat to the ship's company

☑ carry out a full or partial search of the ship.

### 11.3.3 Ship's security level 3

In addition to the above:

☑ Limit access to a single controlled point

☑ allow access only to those responding to the security incident or threat

☑ stop all embarkation and disembarkation

☑ stop all cargo and stores handling

☑ if required, prepare for:
  • evacuation of the ship
  • movement of the ship

☑ prepare for a full or partial search of the ship.

*Note that, at security level 3, the ship should comply with the instructions of those responding to the incident or threat.*

## 11.4   Checklist to Prevent Intruders (Stowaways)

History and experience demonstrate that skilled intruders are, once onboard, extremely hard to find, even on a ship with efficient search procedures.

Therefore, you should develop formalised plans for conducting thorough and extensive searches of the ship for any intruders.

The following precautions should be among those taken while in port:

- ☑ Anchor watch maintained
- ☑ main deck and gangway well illuminated and manned
- ☑ focsle and all storerooms locked
- ☑ hawse/spurling pipe covers fixed in position
- ☑ lifeboat properly secured
- ☑ mooring lines well tended and fitted with large rat guards
- ☑ no pilot ladders etc to be left hanging over the ship's side
- ☑ visitors challenged and identified at the gangway
- ☑ high profile deck watch
- ☑ careful checking of containerised, palletised and other unitised cargoes
- ☑ access doors to the accommodation locked and sealed where possible, without compromising a safe means of escape.

In ports where a pass system is not viable, it will be helpful to maintain:

- ☑ A log with each visitor's name, duties, name and rank of the person visited, and times of boarding and disembarking
- ☑ a running total of the persons boarding and leaving.

The following measures for deterring intruders should be taken prior to departure:

- ☑ A thorough search of all areas of the vessel should be conducted to discover any stowaway who may be onboard. This must be carried out in accordance with the vessel's own search list

☑ where available, professional shore based companies with dogs should be engaged

☑ notices should be displayed at the gangway stating that 'Cargo holds will be treated with gas prior to departure'. This may well act as a deterrent for stowaways who can read and, on departure, compressed air could be injected to give the impression of injecting gas into the holds

☑ the vessel's next port of call should not be displayed unless it is suitably unattractive for a stowaway.

After departure following berthing at certain problematic countries, it is beneficial to stop the vessel within port limits and carry out a further search, including the stores and, if possible, the cargo holds. It is easier to land stowaways that are found if this is done before the vessel has left territorial waters.

All measures taken should be logged as evidence to immigration authorities that all proper precautions were taken.

*Note: In certain ports, there are significant risks of explosive devices being placed onboard. However, it is considered that an efficient stowaway search should be sufficient to detect any such devices.*

## 11.5  Crew Identity

Before beginning the voyage, you must be satisfied that each crew member has full and proper identification that reflects the requirements of the ISPS Code.

Improper or incomprehensible seafarer identification may arouse suspicion of national immigration authorities and could result either in the ship being refused entry to a port or in the immediate repatriation of the crew member concerned.

Should you have any concerns you should contact the company for direction.

# 12 Steering Gear and Engine Tests

Responsible Officer: Master, Chief Engineer and Chief Officer

Action Officers: OOW and Duty Engineer Officer

## 12.1 Responsibilities

- The Master is responsible for choosing a time for steering gear and engine tests to be made prior to arrival at port and prior to the engines being put on standby for any particular passage. Tests should be carried out in consultation with the Chief Engineer
- they will normally be conducted within 24 hours of arrival and, in the case of the USA, 12 hours prior to entering the EEZ.

## 12.2 Steering Test at Sea

☑ At the time and place designated, the engines should be stopped to test the steering gear, provided that the traffic and weather conditions permit

☑ the OOW and the duty Engineer Officer should complete the tests as instructed in the company checklist

☑ on completion of the checklist, it should be signed by the OOW and the duty Engineer Officer and placed in the bridge steering checklist file

☑ should any defect be noted, the Master and Chief Engineer should be advised immediately.

## 12.3  Steering Test in Port

- ☑ In port and prior to sailing, a steering test will take place as part of the gear test
- ☑ because the testing of gear is normally done once cargo operations are completed, and owing to time restrictions, the steering test can be carried out as a separate test within 12 hours of the anticipated sailing time
- ☑ the time of testing should be arranged between the OOW and the duty Engineer Officer
- ☑ the steering checklist must be completed and filed
- ☑ regardless of whether or not this test is completed, the steering will again be tested in hand steering by the bridge during the normal gear test, once cargo operations are completed.

## 12.4  Engine Tests at Sea

- Engine testing should be carried out at the same time as the steering gear tests
- engine tests consist of astern and ahead movements in bridge control mode and under engine room control
- the Chief Engineer may ask for other engine tests to be carried out, such as from the emergency control position
- engine tests must be logged and the engine room movement record from the bridge must be kept.

## 12.5  Engine Tests in Port

- All engine tests in port must be coordinated between the deck and engine departments
- engine tests should, when possible, be arranged with the shore cargo supervisor
- before any engine test, all lines must be tight, cargo equipment clear of any ship obstruction, security of the gangway checked and the propeller clear
- the bridge controls should be manned and should control the test. The OOW on deck must be in constant communication with the bridge during the test and is authorised to halt the test at any time
- the shore cargo supervisor must be advised when the test is completed.

# 13 Ballast Water Management

Ballast water management has now became a matter of international concern and you are advised to obtain detailed information for all ports or countries of call on passage to ensure compliance with their national legislation. Non-compliance with any such legislation could result in fines and/or delays, with claims possibly being made by the charterers against the ship.

Recommendations are contained in the IMO's Resolution 868 from the Twentieth Assembly (A20) on 'Guidelines for the Control and Management of Ship's Ballast Water to Minimize the Transfer of Harmful Aquatic Organisms and Pathogens'.

Although there are no mandatory international regulations, a growing number of countries require:

- ☑ Ballast water exchange prior to arrival
- ☑ clear and documented ballast water exchange procedures
- ☑ production of a ballast water exchange report upon arrival.

Any failure to comply with such requirements will often result in a fine.

Any ballast water exchange must be closely monitored, with contingency procedures in place to deal with any eventualities that may arise.

Any ballast water transfer or operation at sea will require:

- ☑ A plan before commencing any such operations, detailing all stages and confirming the stability of the vessel at each stage
- ☑ effective communication between all personnel involved
- ☑ procedures to be prepared by the company.

You should adhere to the procedures and safety precautions on ballast water exchanges provided in your SMS. These may include:

- Prevention of over/under pressurisation of ballast tanks
- the effect of free surface on stability
- maintenance of adequate intact stability
- permissible seagoing strength limits of shear forces, bending moments and torsional forces
- maximum permitted draughts
- prohibiting weather conditions.

In freezing weather conditions, such operations should be avoided as tank ventilation pipes or the valve on the ballast system could freeze, compromising the safety of the vessel.

# 14 Standing Orders

During the course of a voyage, whether entering port, leaving port, anchoring or during the many other procedures that we carry out, all of us at some time or another forget something, sometimes with considerable consequence.

All Masters are required to write their standing orders and rarely are they the same. They are, or should be, the accumulation of the experience of the Master in situations where he has observed fault or problems that could have been avoided by well laid down orders. Checklists for emergencies have not been included in this section, but will be found, where relevant, throughout this book

## 14.1 Standing Orders (Sea)

### 14.1.1 Responsibilities

- The Chief Officer is head of the deck department and is responsible to the Master for all matters of deck crew, watchkeeping duties and bridge maintenance. He is responsible for maintaining the Deck Log Book and it is essential that this is completed correctly. The basis is that, if you are in doubt, enter your remarks
- the 2nd Officer is the navigation officer and is responsible for all aspects of navigation. He should prepare the passage plan and charts for the forthcoming voyage in good time and advise the Master if there is any additional chart or publication required. He is required to draw the Master's attention to any area on the chart that the ship will pass that might require particular attention. In addition, he must bring to the Master's attention any navigation warning that might affect the ship
- he should advise the times of high and low water throughout the ship's stay in port
- he is responsible for the readiness and good order of the bridge equipment

- prior to arrival in port, he must advise the bridge of any special national or port requirements
- the 3rd Officer is responsible for all signalling equipment and flags. He must ensure that the required flags are ready for use prior to port entry
- he will assist the navigation officer as required
- he must prepare routine port and sea messages
- he is responsible for the maintenance of all portable communications equipment
- he should act as the ship's meteorological (met) officer and ensure that all weather reports are received in a timely fashion and that the ship's position is plotted on the weather charts.

## 14.1.2 Standing orders

- For the purpose of these orders, the following will apply:

  Good visibility: above 5 miles
  Restricted visibility: 2 – 5 miles
  Poor visibility: 1 – 2 miles
  Fog: below 1 mile

- these orders are not comprehensive. They are intended to complement existing professional understanding and the company instructions and guidelines. All officers are expected to use their initiative in following them. They are to be read and acted upon in conjunction with the following:
  - International Convention on the International Regulations for Preventing Collisions at Sea, 1972 (2003 edition)
  - Bridge Procedures Guide, fourth edition 2007
  - company standing orders
  - company SMS
  - the ship security plan
- the Master's attention should be brought to any perceived conflict between his orders and any of the above
- all bridge equipment and controls are there to be used if the circumstances require. All officers are expected to read the instrument manuals provided and have an understanding of the operation and limitation of the instruments

- all navigational equipment and controls are to be tested at least 2 hours prior to departure and the test list completed. As part of this check, the gyro compass and all repeaters, including radar, are to be aligned. Engine room and bridge clocks must be synchronised. The steering gear must be tested in main and secondary modes
- the Master must be advised of the following:
  - any decrease in visibility
  - any malfunction of bridge equipment
  - any doubt whatsoever regarding the safe navigation of the vessel
  - if at any time his presence or advice are required
  - any adverse weather reports
- the Master should expect the OOW to act with common sense regarding the RPM of the vessel. Should the vessel start to pound, the RPM should be reduced as required, at the same time advising the Master
- when making large course alterations, the Master may wish the ship to be put into hand steering. The wheel is not to be handed over during any such alteration until the vessel is steady on the new course. When in traffic that requires a number of alterations, the Master will expect the helmsman to be at the wheel
- when altering course for other vessels, early action must be taken and the alteration substantial, so that there can be no confusion on the other vessel about your intentions. Under normal circumstances, alterations should take place not less than 'x' miles away and ships should not be passed less than 'y' miles away
- no other duties are to interfere with keeping of a responsible lookout. If, at any time, essential work is to be completed by the OOW, he must tell the Chief Officer, who will ensure that adequate lookouts are provided for that work period. Under no circumstance is work to be undertaken by the OOW in regular shipping waters
- the Master's presence on the bridge does not relieve the OOW from his charge. The Master will verbally take the con. If there is any uncertainty about who has command, the OOW must ask the Master for clarification

- irrespective of the Master taking command, the OOW must check the Master's actions, continue with plotting the vessel's position and call the Master's attention to the movement of other vessels or any unsafe navigational procedures he might be taking

- the OOW's prime responsibility is for the safety of the ship and he must take any action required to ensure this. If, at any time, he feels that the ship is standing into danger or he is unsure of the situation, he must call the Master if time allows. Otherwise, he should, without hesitation, take any action required to put the vessel into safety. These actions might include use of helm and engines, change or reversal of course, or stopping the ship until the situation can be resolved

- in the event of an emergency stop at sea, if there is power to the rudder, the ship is to be put onto a course away from any immediate danger. Generally, this should be to steer the ship away from any land or ship in the area

- the OOW is not to take the watch until he is completely satisfied about the ship's position and the safety of the present course. Should there be any dispute about either the position or safety of the ship, the Master is to be called immediately

- in taking any immediate action, if there are other ships in the vicinity and if time permits, they should be alerted through the use of sound signals and/or VHF

- any defect or malfunction of equipment must be entered into the bridge defect book, with the date and time, and sent to the appropriate person or head of department for signature

- if, due to deteriorating weather conditions, the OOW feels that it is unsafe on deck, he must place the decks out of bounds by broadcast and by informing the heads of department. If any personnel are on deck at the time, they are to be ordered into the accommodation

- the Deck Log Book is an important legal document and the OOW must ensure that all entries are properly made, particularly in respect of weather conditions. When the ship is rolling, he should enter the degree of roll together with remarks about any pitching or taking water on deck

- the OOW is responsible for displaying the correct flag and light signals. The ensign must be hoisted at the gaff when the ship is under way and at the stern when the ship is alongside or at anchor
- prior to arrival in port, the OOW must test communications, both bridge and portable. He must also synchronise the clocks between the bridge and engine room. He is responsible for ensuring that the pilot ladder is rigged in good time and that the crew are called to stations ready for arrival.

### 14.1.3 Under pilotage

- When the pilot is on the bridge, he is to be treated with the same courtesy as if he has the rank of Master. The pilot is advisor to the Master for the direction of the ship. His presence on the bridge does not relieve the OOW of any of his responsibilities for the safe navigation of the ship and he must continue with his duties, advising the pilot of any navigation or shipping hazards he feels might endanger the ship
- should the pilot at any time give an order that does not directly concern the navigation of the ship, give any cause for concern, or if he has any complaint regarding any aspect of the ship, the Master is to be informed immediately.

## 14.2  Standing Orders (Port)

Quite often, while the standing orders for sea are comprehensively covered, the same is not true for port. In actual fact, this should be the responsibility of the Chief Officer, under the guidance of the Master. Even if they are written by the Chief Officer, they should be subject to the Master's satisfaction before they are distributed.

These orders are intended to complement those of the Chief Officer. The OOW, in addition to cargo duties, is responsible for the safety and security of the ship and those onboard. To assist in this, the following will apply:

- The OOW must ensure that the ship is held fast alongside and that the mooring lines are adjusted with the rise and fall of the ship
- in the event of the weather deteriorating, the OOW should not hesitate to order additional moorings to be put out to ensure the ship is secure. If required, the outboard anchor may be walked out to the bottom. If there is danger of the ship coming off the berth, the VHF should be used to contact the port and tugs should be ordered to keep the vessel alongside
- the OOW must ensure that the gangway is kept at the correct height to avoid damage, with particular regard for passing vessels, and that the gangway is safe, well lit and secure at all times
- when ships are passing, it is important to ensure that all the mooring lines are tight. Should any damage to the ship or lines occur when a vessel passes, the time and name of the ship should be entered immediately in the deck log and the port authorities advised of the occurrence by VHF. A damage report should then be filed
- safety equipment must be worn by all personnel, both ship and shore, when on the decks
- in the event of any oil spill, the ship's emergency response plan must be followed
- it is important that any oil in the water near the ship is immediately investigated. The engine room should be checked

and any pumping that is taking place stopped until the source of the oil is established. If the oil is from the ship then the emergency response plan must be followed and the harbour authorities immediately advised. If it is not from the ship, the terminal operators must be advised and the agents notified. An immediate entry must be made in the deck log, together with the names of those notified

- any deposits of oil or grease on the decks must be cleared immediately and the area secured until safe for use
- during the hours of darkness, all gangway and deck lights must be switched on and working
- should an accident occur onboard, it is imperative that, if required, shore assistance is obtained as soon as possible. If there is no immediate contact or telephone available, then the port authorities should be contacted on the VHF. The following information should be given:
  - name of ship
  - position in the port
  - nature of the problem and the services required.

An officer should be stationed at the gangway to ensure that, on arrival of the requested services, they can be directed immediately to the accident area.

- In the event of any injury to any person, shore or crew, it is essential that the facts of the accident are recorded as soon as possible. The following details are required:
  - ☑ Nature of injury
  - ☑ treatment given, if any
  - ☑ place and time
  - ☑ lighting conditions
  - ☑ safety equipment worn by the injured person
  - ☑ any suspicion of drug or alcohol use
  - ☑ statements and names of witnesses.

In addition, the company accident form must be completed.

- In the event of any damage occurring to the ship or equipment, a damage report must be filed, signed by the appropriate personnel and an entry made in the deck log

- no shore worker should enter the accommodation except on official business. Any shore worker found in the accommodation must be challenged and either taken to the person they wish to see or requested to leave

- if, at any time, the OOW observes a shore worker behaving in an erratic manner or suspects that they might be under the influence of alcohol or drugs, or that they are working in such a manner that they might cause injury or damage to others or to the ship, then their supervisor must be informed. This must be entered in the deck log. Should their behaviour continue to cause concern, the OOW must request their removal from the ship

- each morning, the deck area in the way of the gangway and accommodation entrance must be washed down and the main deck alleyway cleaned

- flags should be hoisted at 0800 and lowered at sunset

- the bridge equipment checklist must be completed when testing gear prior to departure

- the bridge wings and coamings must be washed down prior to departure, and the bridge windows cleaned

- should the OOW at any time have difficulties, if any accident occurs or there are difficulties with shore personnel, then the OOW must consult with his head of department and the Master if onboard. The Master is to be advised immediately of any accident, damage or pollution incident. In dealing with any member of the ship's company or shore personnel, the OOW is acting on the Master's behalf and with his authority and, provided that he has acted in a responsible manner, will always have the Master's support. All visitors to the ship must be dealt with in a courteous manner, regardless of who or what they are

- the gangway board must state clearly the date and time of departure and the time the crew must be onboard. This must be put on the board at least 24 hours prior to the ship's ETD

- no smoking signs must be displayed and enforced where relevant
- no alcohol is to be brought onto the ship by any crew member or shore worker
- during bunkering, the pollution prevention equipment must be placed out on deck at the bunkering position ready for immediate use and the appropriate signal is to be hoisted. The bunkering checklist must be completed prior to bunkering operations
- the Ship Security Plan must be complied with in line with the requirement of the security level the vessel is at. Any persons onboard who are not identified as bona fide workers must be challenged and identified
- each morning, while in port, the OOW will obtain the weather forecast and bring any change in the weather conditions to the attention of the Chief Officer and the Master.

# 15 Preparation for Port Arrival

If your ship is regularly running between the same ports, preparation becomes automatic and many problems are avoided. Equally, when ships are frequently calling at major ports, completing procedures can be less important because anything missed in one port can be completed in the next. It is when a ship is entering port infrequently, or is entering a port from which it will depart for a prolonged voyage, that port preparation is important, especially if the stay is to be short.

## 15.1 Port Arrival

- ☑ The Navigation Officer must ensure that all relevant navigational warnings are up to date for the port
- ☑ he must ensure that all relevant navigational messages are sent
- ☑ the navigational map of the port must be put into a file on the ARPA computer
- ☑ a tidal table for the duration of the port stay must be made
- ☑ currents in the area of the port approach must be listed and plotted on charts that are suitable for this purpose
- ☑ the Master must note on the chart the positions of 'One hour's notice' to the engine room and standby
- ☑ the OOW must complete the arrival checklist and ensure that the pilot data cards are up to date
- ☑ the OOW must ensure that the correct flags/signals are displayed
- ☑ the intended port approach plan should be laid on the chart
- ☑ where applicable, a security declaration should be sent in advance.

### 15.1.1 Shipboard preparation

- ☑ Anchors cleared away
- ☑ flags hoisted if it is the day of arrival

- ☑ if bunkering, scuppers must be blocked and anti-pollution equipment should be checked and readied
- ☑ store's crane checked
- ☑ covers taken off ropes and windlasses
- ☑ mooring lines and stoppers readied, windlasses tested
- ☑ if advised that the berth is clear, swing gangway out
- ☑ clear decks of lifelines
- ☑ secure fire boxes and stow away lifebuoys
- ☑ secure lifeboats
- ☑ check deck lighting
- ☑ test engines, steering systems and sound signal
- ☑ check communications, fore and aft
- ☑ if the weather is cold, switch on the hydraulics to allow for warm-up time
- ☑ lock non-immediate use hatches and lockers.

### 15.1.2 If anchoring

- ☑ Check anchor lights
- ☑ if required, set a security watch
- ☑ after anchoring, put covers on the hawse pipe
- ☑ tender NOR
- ☑ set engine notice.

### 15.1.3 Information to pass to the agent

- ☑ Your requirements regarding presentation of manifests, etc prior to discharge
- ☑ personnel leaving or joining
- ☑ personnel who require medical or dental treatment
- ☑ fresh water requirements
- ☑ any technical assistance required or technicians that have been requested to attend. It is essential that the equipment is specified, together with the suspected problem or area of concern
- ☑ surveyors requested and what the surveys are
- ☑ what cash is required, together with the denomination of the notes and exchange rates

- ☑ any stores or spares that have been sent to the port, preferably with the shipment number
- ☑ if you have a single crane and will be storing, tell the agent which side the crane is on and request that side alongside in the port
- ☑ request for delivery of charts. If you do not have an appropriate chart for entering the port, arrange through the agent for the pilot to bring it to the ship. The same applies to courtesy ensigns. Order any charts required for the next port, if known
- ☑ bunkers that have been ordered, together with the required time of delivery
- ☑ any special ship peculiarities, such as unusual mooring arrangements or malfunction of navigational equipment
- ☑ for your port emergency listings, you will require the names and telephone numbers of the pollution agencies. At the same time, find out what pollution protection, if any, the port provides
- ☑ quantity of waste for disposal and whether any of it is special or hazardous waste
- ☑ whether the lowering of lifeboats is required
- ☑ what the port regulations are on engine immobilisation
- ☑ ship security state
- ☑ whether the agency representative is attending on arrival
- ☑ when cargo is to commence and which hatches start first.

### 15.1.4 Berth check

- ☑ Is there room for the ship? Ensure the ship's length is known
- ☑ is there any overhang of the ship? Can good leads be given for the mooring lines?
- ☑ what is the locally declared depth on the berth? Is it a safe berth for the ship, ie always afloat
- ☑ cranes and loaders must be clear
- ☑ what fendering is at the berth
- ☑ whether fresh water connections are available
- ☑ whether garbage bins are available
- ☑ what the gangway arrangements are? Shore or ship gangway? Can the safety net be secured ashore?
- ☑ whether the berth is clear of previous cargo residue

☑   on approach, note and log if any oil is in the water in way of the berth (it is advisable to draw this to the attention of the port)

☑   what the berth security arrangements and requirements are.

### 15.1.5 Port documentation

☑   Last port clearance

☑   crew lists

☑   passenger lists (if supernumeraries are onboard, check with the agent whether they can be listed as crew or have to appear on a separate passenger list)

☑   customs forms

☑   health forms

☑   vaccination lists (many ports do not require this - check with the agents)

☑   arms or ammunition

☑   general stores declaration

☑   list of previous ports

☑   dangerous drug list

☑   stores or spares to be landed

☑   security declaration.

The above are the general forms that are required for a port. There could well be local forms required for a specific port and these should be notified to the ship by the agents.

## 15.1.6 Documentation

Before arrival in port, check that the following are up to date and signed:

- ☑ Oil Record Book
- ☑ Garbage Disposal Log Book
- ☑ GMDSS Log Book. Remember this has to be signed daily, not just each page
- ☑ pilot card
- ☑ log books
- ☑ port passage plan
- ☑ hours of work records
- ☑ work permits ready
- ☑ Medical Log Book
- ☑ ship security record.

## 15.2 Port Departure

☑ Under normal circumstances, bridge equipment should be tested at least one hour before the ship is due to sail. This will normally be after cargo operations have been completed

☑ if there is any malfunction, the officer responsible for the maintenance of the equipment must be called immediately to the bridge and the Master informed

☑ the relevant port chart must be ready for use, the port departure plan laid and all navigation instruments ready

☑ currents in the port area must be listed and plotted on charts that are suitable for this purpose.

## 15.3  Preparing for Port Departure

It is surprising just how quickly the last few hours of a ship's stay in port can descend into chaos. Regardless of how well you manage the ship at sea, you do not have much control over all the outside influences in port. A checklist of items to do and reports to receive on your desk can be most useful at such a time:

- ☑  All crew onboard
- ☑  navigation equipment and engines tested
- ☑  all cargo stowed and secured and ship secured for sea
- ☑  ship's certificates returned
- ☑  crew and ship mail posted
- ☑  local currency cash remaining returned
- ☑  ETA given for the next port
- ☑  departure plan prepared
- ☑  pilotage card completed
- ☑  shore hoses disconnected
- ☑  shore loaders/cranes, etc moved from way of the ship
- ☑  garbage landed
- ☑  port clearance given
- ☑  weather report checked
- ☑  tugs and pilot ordered
- ☑  stowaway search completed.

# 16 Insurance and P&I Clubs

The extent of insurance coverage for your ship depends on the scope of cover taken out by your company. A copy of this coverage should be available onboard.

Hull and Machinery (H&M) insurance is insurance of the vessel as the primary asset, covering damages to the vessel, structure, machinery and fittings, and liabilities to third parties arising out of a collision or damage to fixed and floating objects, where not otherwise covered under the P&I coverage. This will be defined by the insurer's Cover Note, and any applicable clauses attached.

## 16.1 P&I Insurance

This covers a shipowner's liability toward third parties. The main areas of the coverage involve:

- Liabilities to third parties arising from collision/damage to fixed and floating objects (generally covering those items not covered under the Hull and Machinery insurance cover)
- personal injury, illness or death
- damage to the marine environment
- cargo damage
- damage to third party property.

The two types of insurance, ie H&M and P&I, interact in the areas of liability in the event of collision or contact damage to third party property.

Under the standard English hull and machinery insurance terms (ITC Hulls – Institute Time Clauses Hulls), collision liability cover has, historically, been limited to 3/4ths of the own ship's liability towards the other vessel in a collision.

Some shipowners have placed full (4/4ths) collision liability with their P&I insurer. This cover would be the most comprehensive liability cover available, as all third party liabilities arising out of the collision would be covered in principle. In such cases, however, the shipowner would still need H&M cover to deal with the loss of or damage to the vessel.

Apart from concern about the damage or injuries that result from an accident, you can be sure that paperwork and blame will also be high on the list. Even if you had nothing to do with the accident or you perceive that it is not the ship's fault, there will be someone trying to prove it is. That is why it is essential that, in any incident that takes place on the ship or involves the ship, if it results in damage to ship, cargo or personnel, the utmost should be done to accurately record all the events, together with any additional information that might help show a complete picture of what happened.

In the event of an incident or allegation that gives, or may give, rise to a third party claim, there are certain actions you should always take and certain actions you should never take.

Always:

- [x] Call your owner or operator
- [x] investigate every allegation of injury or damage
- [x] collect evidence or documentation relating to the incident, including any defective equipment. Store it in a safe place and label the pieces of evidence. Throw nothing away
- [x] take photographs of any damage or circumstances relating to the incident
- [x] instruct witnesses to write a review of what they saw and heard and to draw a diagram if possible. This should be done as soon as possible after the incident. Write personal notes about the incident yourself.

Never:

☑ Allow a surveyor or lawyer onboard the ship or to interview crew members, unless he has identified himself and produced appropriate authorisation to satisfy you that he is acting for your owner or your P&I Club

☑ allow surveyors or lawyers acting for the opposing parties onboard unless you have authorisation to do so

☑ give written material or physical evidence to opposing lawyers and surveyors. If in doubt, do not give anything to anyone or let anyone examine anything

☑ give a personal opinion about who or what was responsible. Keep to the facts. If in doubt, say nothing

☑ allow crew members to express opinions

☑ admit liability, either verbally or in writing

☑ sign a document that you know contains incorrect information. This includes making false entries in log books

☑ think that the problem will go away if you do nothing.

In preparation for the attendance of the P&I Club surveyor, the following could be required:

☑ Witness statements

☑ witnesses standing by for interview

☑ initial assessment of damage

☑ log book entries:
  • date and time
  • nature of damage or injury
  • weather
  • any initial action taken
  • position of the vessel
  • required signatures

☑ copy of the above entries prepared

☑ list of casualties (if any)

☑ details of any medical treatment given

☑ Medical Log Book entry

☑ all relevant ISM procedures and pertinent records

☑    any letters of protest
☑    maintenance schedules, if relevant
☑    all ship's certificates
☑    all officer and crew certificates
☑    copy of the standing orders.

If there is pollution:

☑    Quantity of the pollutant
☑    Oil Record Book
☑    video images/photographs of the extent of the spill (if possible)
☑    all relevant correspondence, emails, etc
☑    samples of the spilled oil, or of any oil collected near own ship, and samples of onboard fuel and oil cargo

*Note: This evidence collection is not applicable for liquefied gas carriers.*

☑    accounts of the incident from all crew members involved
☑    evidence of any previously sighted oil pollution in berth or port area
☑    details of the procedure followed during transfer of cargo or bunkers within the vessel
☑    rates and ullages of loading and/or discharging operations at the time of the spill
☑    a copy of the terminal's cargo or bunker instructions relating to the acceptable loading rate
☑    the name of the crew member in charge of transfer operations
☑    times and results of inspections of equipment used in cargo and bunkering operations
☑    instructions from the owner and/or the charterer
☑    methods of activating emergency stops
☑    procedures in place at the time governing the use of equipment such as scupper plugs and drip trays
☑    any broken equipment whose failure contributed to the spill
☑    whether vessel's ropes/wires are involved
☑    certificates of ropes/wires
☑    records of dates or renewals

- ☑ register of lifting equipment
- ☑ list of relevant contacts and communications made
- ☑ list of actions taken by other parties
- ☑ any statements made by other parties
- ☑ any photographs of the incident and scene of incident
- ☑ lighting conditions at the time of incident.

## 16.2  Letter of Undertaking

You may have to ask that your P&I Club issues a Letter of Undertaking (LOU) to prevent your vessel being arrested.

Such a situation will typically arise when:

- Persons (other than the crew) are injured while onboard
- cargo has been damaged during the voyage
- there has been a pollution incident
- your vessel has been involved in a collision.

Claimants may threaten to arrest the vessel to seek security for their alleged claim.

To prevent any delay to the vessel, the P&I Club usually provides a LOU if certain conditions are met, such as the claim is within the scope of the P&I cover provided, the P&I premiums are paid up to date, etc. However, you should be aware that your P&I Club is not obliged to issue an LOU.

Generally, a claimant will accept an LOU rather than insisting on a bank guarantee as an LOU can be provided within a short period of time, while preparing a bank guarantee can be time consuming.

In the case of a collision, your hull and machinery underwriters will cover 3/4ths of the liability. However, your P&I Club may be requested to provide an LOU to cover liability that will be allotted to your hull and machinery underwriters.

## 16.3  Fines

It will often feel like fines are issued when the port notices even the slightest discrepancy.

Fines may be presented to you for a range of violations, typically including:

- Contravening the international collision regulations or local traffic regulations
- contravening a traffic instruction that was given to the vessel
- out of date certificates
- any irregularities concerning customs forms, manifests or crew lists
- any irregularities concerning declared ship's stores, medical stores (including out of date medicines onboard) or the crew's personal effects
- pollution of the marine environment, including air or sewage
- any perceived breach of MARPOL regulations
- arriving with stowaways onboard.

# 17 Non-Standard Items

## 17.1 Confined Space Entry Checklist

It is a problem that we often misinterpret what an enclosed space is. Too often we think of double bottoms and other tanks as the only enclosed spaces to be concerned about. However, many products and cargoes give off gases of some form or another, some of which are heavier than air, so although we open a space and ventilate the top, the gases below remain. It is therefore essential that all levels of the atmosphere in a tank are tested before entry.

If a tank or space has been cleaned, that does not necessarily mean that the space is free to enter. The materials used to clean the space can also give off gases, so the atmosphere after cleaning could be worse than before.

If you treat any space that has not had entry for some time as an enclosed space, and with suspicion until proven safe by testing, then you cannot go far wrong. The following points must be considered:

- ☑ Is entry necessary?
- ☑ are the atmosphere testing instruments calibrated?
- ☑ check gas tests results are showing $O_2$ levels of at least 20.9%
- ☑ for deep tank, ensure that all levels, especially the bottom of the tank, are monitored before entry
- ☑ all tests are to be recorded
- ☑ ensure that the atmosphere is monitored during period of entry
- ☑ ensure the space has been ventilated in ample time before entry and ventilation continues during entry
- ☑ specify which PPE equipment is required
- ☑ ensure BA equipment is standing by
- ☑ check that person with BA equipment on can enter the space

- ☑ ensure communications are functioning and continuously monitored
- ☑ ensure a crew member is in immediate attendance outside the entrance to the space
- ☑ ensure the entry permit is completed and signed
- ☑ ensure that task evaluation is completed.

## 17.2  War Zones

A war zone can be declared by a Government, an insurance grouping such as the Lloyd's Market Association, which is a group representing the underwriters at Lloyd's, or a shipping group such as the IBF (International Bargaining Forum).

A war zone can be an area in which danger of warlike acts exists or an area in which terrorist or piracy threat has reached such a scale that a war zone designation is warranted.

War zones can therefore range from an area encompassing thousands of square miles of seas in which general war operations are being conducted, to a localised area considered by shipping and/or insurance groups to be at high risk from piracy.

To determine the precautions required, it is sensible to carry out a threat analysis. This would be based on intelligence regarding any aggressive action that poses a threat to the ship.

The threat can be broken down into four main categories, each with their own subdivisions:

Surface

- Gunfire
- missile attack
- FPB (fast patrol boats)
- small arms
- boarding.

Air

- Missile attack
- gunfire
- helicopter
- bomb
- boarding.

Subsurface

- Submarine attack
- mines
- underwater obstacles.

Internal

- Explosives
- piracy
- sabotage.

For many of these threats, the merchant ship is entirely reliant on external support and protection and whatever initiatives and equipment is decided on by their government. There are, however, certain elementary precautions that ships can take when in such areas, and the scale of these precautions should be in proportion to the threat evaluation. Prior to entry into the area, contact other vessels in the vicinity. For a low threat evaluation, such as piracy, an informal convoy system might prove a deterrent.

### 17.2.1 War zone checklist

- ☑ Boat lowered to the embarkation deck and prepared for immediate launch
- ☑ double up the watches
- ☑ lookouts placed on both bridge wings
- ☑ close all watertight and weather doors
- ☑ close down all deadlights, no visible lights other than navigation lights
- ☑ fire hoses run out in the most vulnerable areas
- ☑ distribution of safety equipment around the vessel
- ☑ crew cleared from most vulnerable areas. Places in the ship with tiles or glass should be considered highly dangerous if the threat is from explosives
- ☑ consider engine room manning
- ☑ two steering motors running

- ☑ consider lighting. This will range from blackout for air attack to high visibility as an anti-piracy precaution
- ☑ first aid items placed at strategic points throughout the accommodation
- ☑ muster point established in the safest area of the ship
- ☑ is additional safety equipment required, such as chemical gas masks?
- ☑ pre-entry meeting with crew to discuss the threat and the procedures.

## 17.3 Piracy

There is an increase in violent attacks in certain parts of the world notably:

- East Africa
- West Africa
- South East Asia
- East Coast of South America
- Caribbean Sea (certain areas).

### Somalia, the situation in 2009

Pirates off the Somali coast launch their attacks from so-called mother ships, using small speedboats. The pirates are armed with assault rifles and rocket propelled grenades (RPGs), that are capable of penetrating the ship's hull. The pirates will approach the target in darkness by speedboat, or even in broad daylight, and will then threaten the ship with their RPGs, come alongside and board using grappling hooks, scramble onto the deck with their automatic weapons and take the crew hostage.

After boarding, which is usually effected in international waters, they will normally bring the ship into Somali waters to one of several ports that are essentially pirate safe havens, with Eyl in the Puntland area of Somalia being the most popular. At this point, through intermediaries, they will commence negotiations with the ship's insurers and owners for a ransom payment, which until late 2008 had typically been one million US dollars although more high profile captures of larger vessels, including VLCCs, have seen this ransom demand increase to tens of millions of dollars. In exchange for this payment, they will release the ship and the captive crew. Reports indicate that the Somalians are running this operation as a commercial business and are not harming the crews that they capture, maintaining a commercial interest in 'looking after the goods'.

Based on over one hundred confirmed attacks in 2008 in this region, in half the cases where an attack was detected early, vessels were able to avoid being boarded and captured. There are no reports of successful pirate attacks on ships with speeds of over 16 knots.

The small craft that the pirates are using limit their operations to relatively calm weather and it is perceived to be difficult to operate these craft when the sea is above sea state 3. The drowning of 5 attackers, when escaping with US$3M from a hijacked VLCC in January 2009, was put down to the sea state.

The likelihood of an attack increases in the period immediately after the release of a hijacked vessel.

Ship owner considerations for ships that are transiting or visiting a port in an attack prone area

- ☑ Provide suitable surveillance and detection equipment to assist crews and help protect the ship
- ☑ eliminate or reduce the need to carry large amounts of cash onboard the ship
- ☑ where possible, route ships away from attack risk areas and avoid geographical bottlenecks
- ☑ transit high risk areas in daylight, if possible
- ☑ enhance security watches in anchorages where ships are deemed to have a high risk of attack
- ☑ provide low-light/night vision binoculars for officers and look-outs
- ☑ fix a yacht radar astern to provide valuable radar cover that is able to detect small craft approaching from that direction
- ☑ provide Kevlar jackets and blankets to protect both the crew and sensitive equipment such as oxyacetylene bottles
- ☑ protect the bridge windows by fixing security glass film
- ☑ on vessels that regularly visit attack prone areas, purchase CCTV and physical deterrent devices, such as barbed wire. In certain circumstances, non-lethal weapons may also be appropriate. Infrared detection and alerting equipment may also be utilised

(Note: Where CCTV is implemented, this should record the main access points to the ship's secure areas and the corridors approaching the entrances to key areas and the bridge.)

☑ construct barriers of barbed or razor wire
☑ coat the gunwhales and rounded sheerstrake areas with anti-climb paint
☑ fit a dedicated enhanced group calling system (EGC) receiver for maritime safety information broadcasts. This would provide a receiver that is not used for commercial purposes to ensure no urgent broadcasts are missed.

**General onboard considerations before transiting an attack prone area**

☑ Place dummies at strategic lookout positions around the vessel to help give the impression of a well guarded ship
☑ make constant visible patrols around the vessel, preferably by no less than 2 crew, equipped with powerful hand lamps and portable radios
☑ ensure you have a ship security plan specifically for a piracy/armed robbery attack. The plan should cover:
  • improving surveillance and the use of lighting and detection equipment
  • crew response to a potential or actual attack
  • the radio alarm procedures to be followed
  • the reports to be made after an attack or an attempted attack.

Armed raiders have traditionally targeted valuables, such as:

  • Contents of the ship's safe
  • personal cash from the crew
  • cameras, laptops, MP3 players, etc.

However, recent attack activity, particularly off Somalia, in late 2008 has seen high profile hijacking of merchant tonnage for ransom. In this case, it was organised crime as opposed to the previously experienced acts of petty theft.

☑ Early detection of a likely attack is the most effective deterrent, as a clear demonstration to attackers that the ship has a vigilant and well trained crew will help deter them from attacking the ship. This is the stage at which the security forces of the nearest littoral or coastal State must be informed through the rescue coordination centre (RCC). The ship's crew should be warned and, if not already in their defensive positions, they should move to them and employ evasive manoeuvres. An aggressive response to an attack can increase the risk to the ship and crew

☑ action to prevent the attackers making it on board the vessel is the second line of defence. Attackers will generally try to board the vessel at the lowest accessible point above the waterline – generally the poop deck

☑ if the GMDSS station does not automatically update the position, update it at regular intervals manually

☑ decide whether AIS is to be switched off or left on

☑ use sandbags to protect sensitive equipment located outside of the accommodation

☑ all access doors to the bridge, engine room, steering gear compartments, officers' cabins and crew accommodation should be secured and regularly inspected

☑ windows and portholes that could offer access should be closed tight and deadlights sealed

☑ internal accommodation doors within secure areas, which give access to vital areas such as the bridge, engine room and Master's cabin, should be reinforced/strengthened and have additional control systems and automatic alarms

☑ muster areas should be nominated, preferably a central citadel that is equipped with food and water supplies and external means of communication, where the crew can muster in the event of an attack and communicate their position and head count to the bridge and outside world,

☑ to prevent crew members being seized and threatened by attackers:
   • all crew members not engaged on essential outside duties should remain within a secure area during the hours of darkness

- crew members who need to patrol/work outside of the secure area at night should be in constant contact with the bridge and should have trained in using an alternative route to return to the secure area should an attack occur or have a place where they can take temporary refuge

☑ use the maximum permissible lighting available, provided this does not interfere with the safe navigation of the vessel:

- focsle and lights over the ship's side should be switched on, so long as these do not endanger navigation (Note: ships should not have their deck lights on when underway, as this could lead other ships to presume that you are at anchor)
- astern of the ship, wide beam floodlights can be used
- steaming with the ship's lights blacked out except for navigation lights is a further option. While this may affect the attackers' orientation on approaching the ship, suddenly switching on the ship's lights to dazzle the attackers and alert them to your awareness of their approach may also place the crew at a disadvantage as they will experience a temporary loss of night vision at the most critical time. It is, however, difficult to maintain a total blackout on the typical merchant ship and this will be influenced by external factors such as the level of moonlight

☑ fire hoses have been found to deter boarders as the attacker has to cope with a powerful jet of water (typically 80 psi). The water may swamp their attack craft and possibly damage/stall the engines/electrical systems. Recent success has involved the fitting of a splash plate a short distance from the fire or tank washing hose nozzle mounted on the ship's side bulwark/railing, creating a fanned downward spray/deluge that has discouraged attackers

☑ when attackers are onboard, your actions should focus on:

- securing the greatest level of safety for those onboard the ship
- seeking to ensure that the crew remain in control of the navigation of the ship
- securing the earliest possible departure of the attackers from the ship

The options available to the Master and crew depend on the level of control the attackers have achieved. For example, gaining control of the bridge or engine room or holding crew members hostage means the hijackers can coerce the Master into complying with their wishes.

- ☑ There have been accounts of entire crews being locked up, so consideration should be given to hiding equipment within the likely areas onboard that are capable of holding all of the crew
- ☑ if you can confirm that your crew are safe within a secure area and the attackers are outside of the secure area and do not place the ship at any imminent risk, then you may consider conducting heavy manoeuvres to encourage the attackers to return to their craft
- ☑ carrying and use of firearms is strongly discouraged. Carriage of arms onboard ship may escalate an already dangerous situation. The use of firearms requires special training and aptitudes. In certain ports, killing a national may expose you or the crew to imprisonment or execution should a pirate be killed in a hostile port. This will also increase the risk that the pirates themselves will use firearms, with the possibility that a crew member may be killed or injured
- ☑ you should ask the local agents or P&I correspondent for:
  - any advice on security issues in that particular port or area and the reliability of official security authorities and private firms
  - contact details for the dock, police or security authorities.

**Additional considerations if your ship is visiting a port/ anchorage in an attack prone area (see also section 17.9 stowaway checklist)**

- ☑ If approaching an anchorage where attacks have taken place, you should consider delaying anchoring by slow steaming or taking a longer route to keep well off shore and reduce the period of risk

☑ if you have crew going ashore in ports in attack prone areas, they should be advised not to discuss the ship, her voyage or cargo details with anyone ashore

☑ as attackers may select their targets based on the cargo stipulated on the manifest, you should limit the circulation of cargo plans and associated documents providing information on the cargoes onboard

☑ security guards employed in a port or anchorage should be in contact with their colleagues on different ships and the port authorities. You should only use security firms that have themselves been vetted by the appropriate authorities.

### 17.3.1 Action points onboard

Implementing the ship's security plan

☑ Before entering an attack prone area, train and drill the crew on the alarm signals, procedures and actions in the ship's security plan

☑ all doors allowing access to the bridge, engine room, steering gear and crew accommodation/cabins should be secured and controlled in attack prone areas and should be regularly inspected. On accommodation doors that do not have a key, the lock should be changed. Doors can be temporarily secured by fixing a 3″ x 3″ joist of wood between the deck level and the door handle to secure and prevent opening of the door from outside

☑ secure all lockers to help prevent the attackers gaining access to tools and equipment onboard

☑ train with any surveillance/detection equipment provided onboard.

Watchkeeping in the area

Maintaining a vigilant lookout is essential. There are frequent reports that the first indication of an attack was when the attackers appeared on the bridge or in the Master's cabin. Being vigilant and able to pre-warn of a likely attack gives opportunity to:

☑ Sound the alarm

- ☑ alert other ships and coastal authorities
- ☑ illuminate the approaching craft
- ☑ initiate an evasive manoeuvre.

Clear signs that demonstrate the ship is aware it is being approached have proven to deter attackers.

Give plenty of searoom to small objects, particularly when they show no lights.

Increase the lookout:

- ☑ Bridge watch increased
- ☑ additional lookouts covering the stern or radar 'blind spots' should be considered
- ☑ radar should be constantly manned, although it may be difficult to detect low profile fast moving craft on ship's radars.

Communications:

- ☑ Verbal instructions must be clear
- ☑ use caution when passing information by VHF regarding cargo, valuables or the crew nationality in areas where attacks occur
- ☑ ensure an officer responsible for communications is on duty at all times when the ship is in an attack prone area:
  - maintain a constant listening watch with the appropriate shore or naval authorities when in attack prone areas
  - monitor all maritime safety information broadcasts for the area as INMARSAT's enhanced group calling system (EGC) will normally be issued via the SafetyNET service.

Be alert for small craft matching your speed. Small craft that appear to be matching the speed of the ship on a parallel or following course should always be treated with suspicion as they could close in rapidly to mount an attack.

Where a suspicious craft has been observed, it is important that an effective watch is maintained in case this craft is a distraction with the attackers' intent to approach from a second attack craft rather than the decoy.

## Suspected Attack

☑ If suspicious movements are identified that could indicate an imminent attack, you should contact the appropriate rescue coordination centre (RCC) or radio station that is recommended for that area. A danger message should be transmitted on VHF Channel 70 using the 'safety' priority, with further announcements on a working channel

☑ if AIS has been switched off, it should be switched on

☑ signal projector and beam lights can be used to check suspect craft

☑ when it is apparent that the safety of the ship is threatened:
  • the Master should contact the RCC/Coast Radio Station
  • if appropriate, broadcast an 'All Stations' 'Urgency Message' (PAN-PAN) on VHF Channel 16 or any other radio communications service considered appropriate such as INMARSAT. This should be supplemented by DSC calls on VHF Channel 70 (and/or 2,187.5 kHz) using the 'all ships urgency' category
  • if the urgency signal has been used and an attack doesn't develop, the ship should cancel the message as soon as it knows that action is no longer necessary, again addressing 'all stations'

☑ navigation permitting, heavy wheel movements made as the attackers approach may deter the would-be attackers or make it difficult for them to attach poles or grappling irons to the ship. Attackers' confidence may diminish when faced with a vessel that is making rapid wheel movements.

## Confirmed Attack

☑ Should an attack occur placing the ship and crew in danger and requiring urgent assistance, immediately broadcast a distress message (MAYDAY) using all available radio communications systems. To reduce any delays, if using a ship earth station, you should ensure the CES associated with the RCC is used

☑ alarm signals, including the ship's whistle, should be sounded on the approach of attackers. Announcements or a specific alarm signal that can indicate where the attackers are boarding will assist crew in exposed locations as they determine the best route to a secure area

☑ distress flares should only be used where you consider that the actions of the attackers are putting the ship into imminent danger. Radio transmissions, rather than distress flares, should be used to alert nearby shipping of the risk of attack

☑ from a secure location onboard, the ship may be able to covertly send a message to an RCC. You must be aware that, with the attackers onboard, when the RCC relays the message or attempts to establish communication with the ship, the attackers could become aware that a piracy/attack alert has been transmitted. This may further endanger the lives of the crew onboard.

If the attackers gain control and take hostage(s)

☑ Remain calm
☑ leave the CCTV recording equipment running
☑ if the attackers are willing to negotiate, your objectives should be:

- achieving the safe return of any hostages
- ensuring your crew retain control over the safe navigation of the ship
- helping the attackers make the decision to leave the ship. This can be assisted by assuring them that they have been given everything they demand and that nothing has been hidden

  *(There will, however, be occasions where compliance with the attackers' demands is the only safe option and resistance or obstruction of any kind is patently dangerous)*

☑ if you can confirm that the attackers do not have firearms, rushing at them, in the form of a sortie by a trained crew has, in the past, forced the attackers to leave a ship. A sortie attack by the crew should:

- only be carried out if there is minimal risk to the crew. The sortie party should always stay together
- only be carried out if they significantly outnumber the attackers
- have its chance of success improved by use of water hoses.

Do not:

- Come between the attackers and their craft
- seek to capture attackers. However, if you do apprehend an attacker, he should be placed in secure confinement and cared for as you would a stowaway, notifying the coastal State at the first opportunity.

### Attackers leave the ship

If the crew are in a secure position, it is unwise to leave the safety of this position until it is verified that the attackers have left the ship. A signal known to the crew on the ship's whistles and alarm bell can be used to signify the 'all clear'.

Piracy Reporting Centre (PRC)

If you are attacked, you should report the attack to the PRC of the International Maritime Bureau (IMB) in Kuala Lumpur, Malaysia. The Centre can be contacted on a 24 hour basis.

Tel:  + 60 3 2078 5763
Fax: + 60 3 2078 5769
Telex: MA34199 IMBPCI
Email: imbkl@icc-ccs.org or piracy@icc-ccs.org
24 Hours Anti-Piracy HELPLINE Tel: + 60 3 2031 0014

## 17.4  Hot Work in Cargo Oil Tanks

Before hot work is carried out, a formal risk assessment must be conducted by those who will be involved.

Precautions to be taken before carrying out hot work in cargo oil tanks should include the following:

☑  Cargo oil tanks where hot work is to be carried out must be water washed and gas freed and any flammable material must be removed

☑  adjacent or surrounding tanks must be water washed and gas freed and any flammable material must be removed or moved away from the bulkheads and structures adjacent to cargo oil tanks where the hot work is to be carried out

☑  apart from the designated slop tank that contains residual pipeline and tank washings, all other cargo oil tanks on the tanker should be either purged or water washed and gas freed

☑  cargo oil tanks that have been water washed and gas freed should be blanked from the IGS distribution main

☑  cargo suction pipelines that interconnect gas free and non-gas free cargo oil tanks should be washed and charged with clean water

☑  cargo valves should be set so that cargo oil tanks are isolated by at least two valves. The designated slop tank should be isolated by as many valves as possible

☑  the designated slop tank should be isolated from the IGS distribution main by closing the IG isolation valve

☑  cargo oil tanks that have been purged should be isolated from the IGS distribution main by closing their IG isolation valves

☑  pressure in the designated slop tank and purged cargo oil tanks must be closely monitored, and should be maintained at about 200 mmWG (20 mb or 2 KPa)

☑  heating coils should be blown through with compressed air and positively isolated by blanking

☑  hydraulic pipelines in a tank, as part of the cargo valve control or pumping system, should be depressurised and, in the area of the hot work, they should be protected with heat retardant coverings. Isolation valves should be closed. Hydraulic pumps or power packs should be isolated and an electrical isolation certificate issued. If hot work is to be carried out near to the hydraulic pipelines, a risk assessment must be made to identify the control measures necessary to prevent ignition of hydraulic oil

☑ the mast riser vent valve should be kept open so that the accumulation of hydrocarbon gas in the IGS distribution main is avoided

☑ if there are no slops onboard, when all the tanks have been water washed and gas freed and all sections of the cargo pipeline system have been thoroughly water washed and either drained or left full of clean water, sections of the pipeline should be left open to allow ventilation

☑ when hot work is to be carried out on deck above a cargo oil tank or on the vertical side of the hull, then that tank must be prepared in the same way as if hot work was to be carried out in it

☑ the permit issued for hot work should be supplemented with a plan showing the location of the hot work and detailing the precautionary, control and monitoring arrangements that are in place. Conditions where the permit is no longer valid should be made clear.

## 17.5  Heavy Weather (Port)

It is sometimes surprising how, with all our attention to weather at sea, we can let ourselves be lulled into a relaxation of this attentiveness just because we are alongside. A ship is often more vulnerable in port than at sea and it is better to prepare for that vulnerability, even if it does not happen:

- ☑ All lines should be out and doubled up where possible
- ☑ all lines should be tight, with crew standing by to slacken as required
- ☑ when appropriate, stop cargo operations and close the hatches or disconnect the hoses
- ☑ have any shore cargo loaders or cranes moved from the vicinity of the ship
- ☑ ensure that all loose gear on the decks is cleared away and stowed, including cargo residue
- ☑ stop all shore leave
- ☑ if required, request a standby tug
- ☑ put the engines on standby
- ☑ if you are a light ship, and there is enough draught, ballast down as much as possible
- ☑ if the bottom is clear and shallow enough, consideration can be given, depending on the severity of the approaching weather, to ballasting down sufficient to place the ship on the bottom
- ☑ if you are a smaller vessel, consider putting the inboard cable ashore around a bollard
- ☑ lower the outboard anchor to the bottom
- ☑ check whether the port has any available storm lines
- ☑ take down flags and ensigns
- ☑ if necessary, hoist the gangway clear of the berth
- ☑ when all precautions have been taken, this should be logged.

## 17.6  Heavy Weather (Sea)

Heavy weather at sea is preferable to heavy weather in port as at least you have room to manoeuvre your ship.

Crew and passengers have, on occasion, been lost overboard in heavy weather conditions.

You should, on entering heavy weather:

- ☑ Prevent crew or passengers from accessing the deck and exposed areas
- ☑ prohibit working on deck except for essential safety operations
- ☑ make a tannoy announcement covering these items to crew and passengers.

Another large advantage is that, apart from exceptional cases, you are warned about what is coming and have time to prepare your ship and crew:

- ☑ Check that the windlass and anchors are well secured
- ☑ ensure that all forward mooring lines are stowed below or lashed and covered securely on their drums
- ☑ if, after mooring, lines cannot be stowed below then they should be lashed securely to the ship's structure and covered
- ☑ any focsle hatch openings must be secured tight and a rope web lashing put over the cleats
- ☑ all hatch tops and entry points must be checked and the retaining cleats tightened
- ☑ remove lifebuoys and liferafts from open deck positions forward and stow away
- ☑ check the lashings of all deck cargo
- ☑ ensure that all the vents are covered and well lashed down
- ☑ all weather doors in exposed areas are to be battened down
- ☑ tighten and secure all halyards
- ☑ check the mast stays
- ☑ remove all loose gear from the decks

- ☑ if intending to run before the seas, ensure that the poop deck is clear
- ☑ rig lifelines if they are not already rigged
- ☑ check all deck lights are ready for use
- ☑ warn all departments in ample time to ensure they secure their stores and work places
- ☑ ensure that all furniture in public rooms is secured
- ☑ have engines on standby in ample time
- ☑ if close to land, consider finding a lee
- ☑ if on a weather shore, stand clear of the land as much as possible before the onset of the weather
- ☑ if at anchor, heave it and ride out the weather at sea. Your anchor is not designed to be used in extreme weather conditions
- ☑ do full engine and steering checks prior to the onset of heavy weather
- ☑ be prepared to go to hand steering at any time required
- ☑ place all external decks out of bounds, except in an emergency
- ☑ check windscreen washers, wipers and clear view screens
- ☑ have searchlights trained forward to enable you to see the seas over the bow and the fore part of the ship
- ☑ adjust speed and course for the best way of the ship
- ☑ ensure that all vessels in the immediate vicinity are kept advised of your intentions
- ☑ rearrange crew to ensure adequate bridge team cover to meet hours of rest requirements.

## 17.7  Freezing Conditions

You don't have to go into ice bound areas with ice class ships to encounter freezing conditions. They can occur in severe winter conditions in many places around the world such as Korea, China, the North Sea and the Barents Sea. Nor does the sea have to be frozen to freeze your fresh water pipes and tanks. If you do not take precautions in such areas, severe damage can result.

When developing plans and ship specific checklists for entering cold weather or areas of ice, the following objectives should be considered:

- ☑ Obtaining available weather and ice reports prior to entering the area
- ☑ notifying the departments onboard of the approaching conditions and likely hazards
- ☑ maintaining the sea suctions, rudder and propeller immersed
- ☑ limiting the vessel's trim
- ☑ reducing ice flows when manoeuvring and berthing
- ☑ preventing hull plate damage (by reducing speed)
- ☑ preventing rudder and propeller damage by avoiding astern engine movements
- ☑ avoiding anchoring
- ☑ verifying the hull integrity (from the soundings of all tanks and spaces)
- ☑ maintaining clear walkways (using scrapers and salt or sand)
- ☑ ensuring there is suitable PPE for all crew
- ☑ making the crew aware of the dangers of exposure
- ☑ ensuring that all unused piping is properly drained
- ☑ ensuring that any unused steam winches are disengaged, turning slowly and lubricated as necessary
- ☑ ensuring that all heating coils are suitably drained and blown through when not in use.

If you are going into an area in winter where there is a chance of you encountering freezing conditions, there are certain precautions that you must consider taking, depending on the severity of the expected conditions.

The following represent lists of items to be checked:

## 17.7.1 Checklist for the Deck Department

The following represents a list of items to be checked prior to entering ice or carrying out ice operations:

- ■ General
- ☑ Check the inventory of cold weather gear onboard and replenish any deficiencies
- ☑ it the ships is not fitted with double glazing, perspex or cling film placed over windows can help insulate the accommodation
- ☑ examine towing fittings on focsle and ensure that a suitable messenger is available to pick up a bridle or towline
- ☑ ensure regular monitoring of the water level in all spaces and compartments. This could be as frequently as hourly in an areas of heavy ice concentrations. This should also be instigated after a strong ice impact
- ☑ searchlights fitted and tested
- ☑ pilot ladders should not be lowered too early as ice can accumulate from spray
- ☑ ships hydraulic systems filled with a fluid suitable for cold weather operations. Ships fitted with tunnel thrusters should not use these as they are liable to damage from ingested ice, resulting in damaged blades

- ■ Deck service lines

Isolate and drain the following lines, leaving the drains open:

- ☑ Fire mains. Valves must be left cracked open
- ☑ general service line and fresh water line to all deck outside taps
- ☑ deck air line
- ☑ chain locker eductor
- ☑ anchor wash lines
- ☑ winch cooling lines
- ☑ all external taps
- ☑ drain bridge window wash systems unless anti-freeze has been added

☑    be alert for the formation of ice at any overboard discharges and the resultant impact

■    Whistles
☑    Drain main and forward whistles and close drain cocks

■    Safety Gear
☑    Stow forward liferaft and LSA gear
☑    stow deck foam and water fire extinguishers in heated areas
☑    stow lifebuoys

■    Lifeboats
☑    Drain fresh water tanks
☑    ensure portable fresh water tanks are full and located in a warm room nearby
☑    fit lifeboat drain plugs

Consider the addition of:

☑    Sets of sub-zero temperature insulated clothing (S, M and L sizes) including hooded jackets, trousers, gloves and boots
☑    sets of thermal underwear and socks
☑    sets of face masks and goggles
☑    sleeping bags (down filled)
☑    Arctic type igloo shaped survival tents
☑    additional high energy food supplies such as chocolate bars

■    Grease
Grease should be applied liberally to all the moving parts on the decks including:

☑    Windlasses
☑    mooring winches
☑    cargo winches
☑    engaging clutches
☑    pins
☑    operating handles
☑    brake clamping bolt threads

- ☑ all nipple points
- ☑ sounding pipe cap threads
- ☑ hatch dogs
- ☑ davits
- ☑ cranes

Note: A little anti-freeze is effective when mixed into the grease.

- ◼ Halyards and stays
- ☑ If halyards are left up then they should be slacked down

- ◼ Protection
- ☑ Covers off all searchlights
- ☑ covers on hatch control boxes
- ☑ covers on all fire hydrants
- ☑ covers on all fire hose boxes
- ☑ covers on all mooring lines on drums, leaving lashings clear before making fast to enable release
- ☑ covers on bunkering sounding pipes
- ☑ grease and burlap (hessian) hatch drive motors and gypsies

- ◼ Heaters
- ☑ Focsle fan and space heaters switched on
- ☑ winch hydraulic header tank and hatch hydraulic heaters switched on
- ☑ anti-condensation heaters on hydraulic systems switched on
- ☑ winch, hatch pump and exhaust fan motor heaters switched on
- ☑ any deckhouse space heaters switched on
- ☑ fire pump and davit heaters switched on
- ☑ space heaters in emergency headquarters switched on

- ◼ Additional items for tankers
- ☑ Decontamination showers and eyewash stations to be accessible to crew in all weather conditions
- ☑ drain foam lines
- ☑ cargo heating coils either to be empty or steam to be circulated
- ☑ aft peak tank to be heated, if ballasted

☑ pressure vacuum (P/V) breaker to have the correct amount of anti-freeze (glycol)

☑ steam to be opened to deck water seal and cargo oil pump separators

☑ crude oil wash (COW) lines and COW machine stand pipes to be drained

☑ P/V valves to be operated to ensure free movement

☑ insulate lines from cold with a trace-heating system. Care should be taken that thermostats are functional and have enough power to run through cables to provide effective trace-heating

■ Tankers – cargo heating systems

If cargo heating system is not required:

☑ Drain/blow through inlet/exhaust lines to remove all presence of water

If cargo heating is required:

☑ Introduce steam to the cargo heating system before encountering freezing temperatures

☑ consider fitting a small diameter line (jumper line) between the supply and return manifolds on the forward tanks to prevent freezing of the exhaust returns

☑ test all steam and exhaust valves for tightness so as to prevent leakage into 'dry lines'

☑ maintain heating until ship reaches warmer climates

☑ blow through all coils/lines with air immediately after turning off the steam

■ Additional items for gas carriers

☑ Drain both deck water spray/sprinkler lines and safety relief valve drains

☑ drain both safety relief valves and vent masts

☑ cargo heaters and cargo condenser fresh water cooling systems to be kept on continuous circulation. Suitable anti-freeze is to be added

- ☑ emergency eye wash and decontamination shower lines and tanks to be drained
- ☑ attach and post a pipeline drawing of the number and location of the drains and indicate which drains are to be blanked and drained. The same is to be clearly marked at their location
- ☑ isolation valves of lines to be posted and clearly marked at their location
- ☑ if space heaters are not provided, cluster-lights may be safely rigged close to the machinery and electrical panels and kept on

- ■ Note for dry cargo ships

Ships regularly trading in ice should carry a long-handled blow torch fired by propane and a sufficient stock of cylinders should be maintained onboard.

## 17.7.2 Checklist for the Engine Department

The engine room should not be left unattended in ice covered waters.

- ■ General
- ☑ Ensure there is sufficient fuel and FW for at least 7 days extended manoeuvring when approaching Canadian waters
- ☑ can trace heating lines be utilised?
- ☑ are combustion air preheating systems operational for diesel engine jacket water heaters and other systems as applicable?
- ☑ compartment space heater switched on
- ☑ change over to ballast seawater recirculating tank (if fitted)
- ☑ oil tank heaters on (keep steam valve cracked open to prevent bursting of pipe)
- ☑ keep all steam tracing lines active
- ☑ heat-up diesel oil settling and service tank to 30°C
- ☑ clean diesel oil filters daily to prevent wax accumulation
- ☑ lub oil and heavy oil purifiers to be run continuously
- ☑ keep sterntube cooling water tank slack (after peak)
- ☑ oily water separator to be drained of all water if exposed
- ☑ regular check of the stern glands to determine whether water is passing through

- ■ Domestic/sanitary system
- ☑ Monitor domestic fresh water pumps, since continuous running is an indication of ruptured piping
- ☑ watch the fresh water tank levels
- ☑ crack the steam on fresh water tank coils
- ☑ circulate fresh water continuously to eliminate any possibility of freezing
- ☑ maintain a small flow of water through the sanitary system and soil drains
- ☑ if the ambient space temperature falls below 5°C (41°F), apply heating to the sanitary holding tank and the overboard line. If time permits, purge air or steam through all wash water outlets that do not drain to a level well below the water line. If necessary, either add a small amount of anti-freeze (environmentally safe) or salt to unused drain traps and toilets, or insert rubber hoses for easy of future removal

- ■ Ventilation
- ☑ Reduce ventilation and/or provide shields to avoid any direct cold airflow against control and gauging equipment and also small diameter piping systems
- ☑ with a diesel-driven ship, the closing of dampers and a reduction in the ventilation will not create a higher than normal vacuum to build-up inside engine room spaces

  *Recirculation of air in the engine room should be avoided as this will result in a build-up of aromatic hydrocarbon and noxious gases*

- ☑ close funnel flaps as required
- ☑ stop engine room vent fans and/or close distribution flaps as conditions dictate
- ☑ leave the funnel skylights open to maintain funnel circulation (ensure funnel temperature is kept above freezing)
- ☑ use engine room fan heaters as required

- ■ Auxiliary boiler
- ☑ Run on back-up if steam demand makes it necessary

- ■ Main engine seawater system
- ☑ Maintain seawater temperature at inverter (45°F or 7.2°C)
- ☑ activate seawater recirculation system by recirculating to low seachest and/or pump suction as required
- ☑ monitor suction and discharge pressures of seawater pumps and carry out steam injection if any signs of ice formation are noticed in sea chest. This is determined by pressure/flow fluctuations. Steam injection hoses to be kept ready. Open steam to sea chests and the overboard discharge valve, if required

- ■ Hydraulic pumprooms
- ☑ Ship's hydraulic systems should be filled with fluid intended for cold weather operation
- ☑ space heater switched on
- ☑ oil tank heater switched on
- ☑ close compartment vent or use a shield
- ☑ use 70% isopropyl alcohol to remove moisture in hydraulic oil and assist the movement of the controls

- ■ Steering gear flat compartment
- ☑ Space heater switched on
- ☑ if no space heater is available, run hydraulic pumps continuously and use oil suitable for low temperatures
- ☑ oil tank heater switched on
- ☑ close compartment vent or use a shield

- ■ All under-deck passages and duct keel
- ☑ Space heater switched on
- ☑ close compartment vent or use a shield

- ■ Bow thruster room
- ☑ Space heater switched on
- ☑ oil tank heater switched on
- ☑ close compartment vent or use a shield

- ■ Emergency Generator Room
- ☑ Fuel: use winter grade oil

*SOLAS II-1, Reg. 44 states: Emergency generating sets should be capable of being readily started in their cold condition at a temperature of 0°C. If this is impracticable, or if lower temperatures are likely to be encountered, provision acceptable to the Administration should be made for the maintenance of heating arrangements, to ensure ready starting of the generating sets*

☑ add anti-freeze (suitable to minus 40°C) to generator and compressor
☑ close the external vents
☑ any fresh water lines to be blanked off
☑ radiator vents must be open for recirculation
☑ space heater switched on

■ Double bottom tanks
☑ Transfer maximum heavy fuel oil up to the wing tanks
☑ isolate unused heating coils and blow through with air or leave steam on and ensure returns maintained warm
☑ turn on bilge tank heating coil, unless tank is empty

■ Fire main
☑ Put the pump suction on a low seachest
☑ drain the fire main down to sea level
☑ leave the fire pump suction and discharge valves open

■ Deck air
☑ Isolate deck service air at the engine room valve and drain the line
☑ ensure that air to control air and whistle is moisture free

■ Sea inlets
☑ Reduce quantity of seawater pumped into cooling system to reduce blockage by ice
☑ monitor pressure of seawater at inlet and clean strainer as necessary.

### 17.7.3 Ice Accretion

Despite the best precautions, in many areas weather conditions can change quickly causing ice accretion leading to dangerous situations such as list, negative metacentric height (GM) and angle of loll. Accretion can occur through any of the following freezing on the ship's structure:

- ☑ Rain
- ☑ sea spray, with sea temperature less than -1°C
- ☑ shipping seas
- ☑ water leakages from burst pipes or tanks
- ☑ freezing fog.

It is important that all possible precautions are taken, including:

- ☑ Ensuring full compliance with ice accretion allowance stability requirements
- ☑ maintaining a close watch on weather forecasts
- ☑ increasing the frequency of meteorological observations
- ☑ monitoring the icing effects and build-up
- ☑ reviewing voyage plan to consider more sheltered areas.

Should the level of ice build-up cause concern, then the following actions will help alleviate the situation:

- ☑ Reduce speed
- ☑ adjust course to run with wind, reducing relative wind speed
- ☑ head to warmer areas
- ☑ seek a lee from land to reduce wind spray
- ☑ report any unforecasted ice or freezing conditions
- ☑ inform all vessels in the area.

## 17.8  Refugees

If you pick up refugees, your P&I Club should be contacted.

The refugees may have been at sea for a number of weeks and could be suffering from any or a combination of the following:

- Exposure
- hunger
- dehydration
- seasickness
- fatigue.

The United Nations High Commission for Refugees (UNHCR) has issued 'Guidelines for the Disembarkation of Refugees', which details a scheme for the reimbursement of certain costs involved in the landing of refugees. However, this scheme may not cover a deviation for the purpose of landing the refugees. You should therefore consult with your company, provided time allows, if you are considering deviating the vessel.

### Action to be taken

In addition to any other guidance onboard, when refugees are picked up onboard your vessel:

- ☑ Obtain medical advice from ashore if required (administer rehydration salts and possibly suncreams)
- ☑ prepare provisions for the refugees
- ☑ prepare accommodation onboard, including blankets and beds
- ☑ notify your company and P&I Club
- ☑ the Company Security Officer (CSO) will inform the appropriate authorities
- ☑ once a decision is made to land the refugees, inform the company's agent and P&I correspondent.

The following information should be provided to the company and the P&I Club:

- ☑ Date/time and position when the refugees were picked up
- ☑ ETA at next port of call
- ☑ ETA at nearest suitable port if the vessel deviates to land the refugees
- ☑ personal details of the refugees
- ☑ medical condition of the refugees and any medical assistance required.

The following evidence is required in connection with a deviation to land refugees:

- ▪ Date/time and position when the refugees were picked up
- ▪ date/time and position where the vessel deviated from her scheduled course
- ▪ fuel ROB at the time of deviation
- ▪ fuel used for the deviation
- ▪ record of all communication expenses
- ▪ copies of all relevant log books.

## 17.9   Stowaways

Where stowaways are found onboard, your P&I Club should be notified. They will prepare for identification and repatriation of the stowaways.

Initial actions

☑  The stowaway should be treated humanely and not threatened with any violence whatsoever

☑  place the stowaway in a locked cabin (he should not be allowed to wander about the vessel)

☑  if more than one stowaway has been discovered, they should, where possible, be accommodated separately

☑  the place where the stowaway was discovered should be searched for further stowaways and any documents/personal effects/drugs

☑  the place where the stowaway was discovered should be photographed or video recorded

☑  the stowaway should be asked/searched for identity papers (such papers must be confiscated as stowaways often try to hide their identity or destroy their papers)

☑  the stowaway should be thoroughly searched for drugs

☑  the stowaway should be questioned at length as to where and when he boarded

☑  if there is more than one stowaway, question them individually to determine whether they knew each other prior to boarding

☑  question them as to the circumstances under which voluntary return may be possible

☑  explain that if economic/monetary reasons are behind the stowing away, no country will accept him and his repatriation will be inevitable

☑  if you cannot communicate with the stowaway, an interpreter should be engaged.

**Evidence to be collected**

- ☑ Date/time and port where stowaway came on board
- ☑ date/time and position when the stowaway was discovered
- ☑ location where the stowaway was discovered
- ☑ period that the stowaway was hidden
- ☑ medical/physical condition of the stowaway
- ☑ security/gangway watch in place at the port where the stowaway boarded
- ☑ details of those on watch when the stowaway boarded
- ☑ whether shore guards were employed at the port where the stowaway boarded and, if so, details of the company
- ☑ details of the stowaway search conducted prior to departure and details of any stowaways found during that search and where they were delivered ashore
- ☑ records of the care/treatment given to the stowaway (frequency/ type of meals, accommodation, sanitary provisions and times allowed for excercise).

# 18 Handover Arriving/Leaving

When you arrive at your relief port, there is a tendency to relax and then, with the new Master just about to arrive or even already onboard, try to get everything together, pack and hand over in a few hours. No wonder so many times things are left behind, work is not completed and some important handover advice not given. Even safe keys have had to be posted back to the ship! Just a little preparation a few days before can avoid this last minute rush:

- ☑ Final portage account completed
- ☑ cash required drawn and remaining cash itemised
- ☑ safe keys and combination handed over
- ☑ ship's trading documents listed detailing validity, expiry date, renewals and extensions
- ☑ continuous synopsis record up to date
- ☑ list of documents with the agent
- ☑ bond listed and, if possible, checked and agreed
- ☑ list of drugs
- ☑ any ship's weapons and stowage.

Sign the following:

- ☑ Log books
- ☑ ISM documents
- ☑ GMDSS
- ☑ Oil Record Book(s)
- ☑ Garbage Disposal Log Book
- ☑ sign off members of crew who are also leaving
- ☑ your documents collected
- ☑ discharge books
- ☑ certificates
- ☑ entry of handover made in Log Book and signed.

## 18.1  Handover Notes for Incoming Master

Prepared, including:

- ☑ Cargo charter party information
- ☑ bunker fuel and water state
- ☑ fuel and water consumption
- ☑ budget status
- ☑ equipment out-of-order or needing attention
- ☑ repairs ordered or needed
- ☑ crew joining/leaving
- ☑ personnel status
- ☑ exchange rates in use
- ☑ victualling accounts if no Chief Steward
- ☑ charts in order or ordered, plus other related items such as digital chart correction service or digital charts, ie 'Admiralty Vector Chart Service'
- ☑ next port advice
- ☑ inspection and surveys
- ☑ any survey deficiencies still uncorrected
- ☑ critical equipment status for:
    - ☑ engines/propulsion
    - ☑ cargo/equipment
    - ☑ navigation equipment
    - ☑ fire fighting equipment
    - ☑ lifesaving equipment
    - ☑ mooring/anchoring equipment
- ☑ agent contact address for next port
- ☑ cabin keys handed over
- ☑ leave a full refrigerator!

## 18.2  Transferring Command

The Master signing off retains command until he is ready to disembark.

Up until this time, the relieving Master will be ensuring that the vessel is in a seaworthy condition and that there are sufficient bunkers, stores, provisions, water, etc onboard for the forthcoming voyage, plus an allowance for a safety margin. The relieving Master will also ensure that all navigational equipment, machinery, mooring equipment and LSA/FFE equipment is in good working order before sailing.

Each Master will complete all Flag State required log book entries and associated documentation, where applicable. When the Master signs the Log Book, command is officially transferred. In practice, this is done as close as possible to the time the Master signing off disembarks from the vessel.

## 18.3 Certificates/Documents Required to be Carried Onboard Ships

### 18.3.1 On all ships

- ☑ Certificate of Registry
- ☑ International Tonnage Certificate
- ☑ International Load Line Certificate
- ☑ International Load Line Exemption Certificate
- ☑ ship stability booklet/damage control plans
- ☑ safe manning document
- ☑ certificates of competency for Masters, officers and ratings including relevant endorsements
- ☑ medical certificates
- ☑ records of seafarers' hours of work/rest and a schedule of shipboard working arrangements
- ☑ International Oil Pollution Prevention Certificate
- ☑ Oil Record Book
- ☑ Shipboard Oil Pollution Emergency Plan (SOPEP)
- ☑ International Sewage Pollution Prevention Certificate
- ☑ International Air Pollution Prevention (IAPP) Certificate
- ☑ fire control plans/wallet/operational booklet
- ☑ record of onboard training and drills
- ☑ garbage management plan
- ☑ Garbage Disposal Log Book
- ☑ voyage data recorder, compliance certificate
- ☑ cargo securing manual
- ☑ copy of company ISM Document of Compliance
- ☑ Safety Management Certificate
- ☑ International Ship Security Certificate (ISSC) or Interim certificate
- ☑ Ship Security Plan and associated records
- ☑ Continuous Synopsis Record (CSR)
- ☑ Declaration of Security (DOS)
- ☑ record of ship security levels.

## 18.3.2 Passenger ships

In addition to the certificates listed in 18.3.1, passenger ships shall carry:

- ☑ Passenger Ship Safety Certificate
- ☑ Exemption Certificate
- ☑ Special Trade Passenger Ship Safety Certificate
- ☑ Special Trade Passenger Ship Space Certificate
- ☑ search and rescue cooperation plan
- ☑ list of operational limitations
- ☑ decision support system.

## 18.3.3 Cargo ships

In addition to the certificates listed in 18.3.1, cargo ships shall carry:

- ☑ Cargo Ship Safety Construction Certificate
- ☑ Cargo Ship Safety Equipment Certificate
- ☑ Cargo Ship Safety Radio Certificate
- ☑ Cargo Ship Safety Certificate
- ☑ Exemption Certificate
- ☑ document of authorisation for the carriage of grain
- ☑ certificate of insurance or other financial security in respect of civil liability for oil pollution damage
- ☑ certificate of insurance or other financial security in respect of civil liability for oil pollution damage
- ☑ enhanced survey report file
- ☑ record of oil discharge monitoring and control system for the last ballast voyage
- ☑ cargo information
- ☑ bulk carrier booklet.

### 18.3.4 Ships carrying noxious liquid chemical substances in bulk

In addition to the certificates listed in 18.3.1 and 18.3.3, where appropriate, any ship carrying noxious liquid chemical substances in bulk shall carry:

- ☑ International Pollution Prevention Certificate for the Carriage of Noxious Liquid Substances in Bulk
- ☑ survey report file
- ☑ ship structure access manual
- ☑ cargo record book
- ☑ Procedures and Arrangements Manual (P & A Manual)
- ☑ Shipboard Marine Pollution Emergency Plan for Noxious Liquid Substances.

### 18.3.5 Chemical tanker

In addition to the certificates listed in 18.3.1 and 18.3.3, where appropriate, any chemical tanker shall carry:

- ☑ Certificate of Fitness for the Carriage of Dangerous Chemicals in Bulk
- ☑ International Certificate of Fitness for the Carriage of Dangerous Chemicals in Bulk.

### 18.3.6 Liquefied gas carriers

In addition to the certificates listed in 18.3.1 and 18.3.3, where appropriate, any gas carrier shall carry:

- ☑ Certificate of Fitness for the Carriage of Liquefied Gases in Bulk
- ☑ International Certificate of Fitness for the Carriage of Liquefied Gases in Bulk.

## 18.3.7 High-speed craft

In addition to the certificates listed in 18.3.1, 18.3.2 or 18.3.3, where applicable, any high-speed craft shall carry:

- ☑ High-Speed Craft Safety Certificate
- ☑ Permit to Operate High-Speed Craft.

## 18.3.8 Ships carrying dangerous goods

In addition to the certificates listed in 18.3.1 and 18.3.3, where applicable, any ship carrying dangerous goods shall carry:

- ☑ Document of compliance with the special requirements for ships carrying dangerous goods.

## 18.3.9 Ships carrying dangerous goods in packaged form

In addition to the certificates listed in 18.3.1 and 18.3.3, where applicable, any ship carrying dangerous goods in packaged form shall carry:

- ☑ Dangerous goods manifest or stowage plan.

There are other certificates/documents whose carriage is not mandatory. These include:

- ☑ Special Purpose Ship Safety Certificate
- ☑ Certificate of Fitness for Offshore Support Vessels
- ☑ Diving System Safety Certificate
- ☑ Dynamically Supported Craft Construction and Equipment Certificate
- ☑ Mobile Offshore Drilling Unit Safety Certificate
- ☑ Wing-in-ground Craft Safety Certificate
- ☑ Permit to Operate WIG Craft
- ☑ Noise Survey Report.

## 18.4  On Taking Over

On taking over, you should obtain as much information as possible from the Master signing off. You should, as thoroughly as time permits, familiarise yourself with the vessel. This is best described as:

- ☑  Knowledge of your duties
- ☑  understanding the vessel
- ☑  understanding the company's systems and procedures.

Questions to ask the outgoing Master:

- ☑  Portage account. Run through it with him and see his final account for handover
- ☑  consummables, fuel and water for the next voyage
- ☑  his assessment of Officers and key ratings, especially the Chief Officer, Chief Engineer, watchkeepers and Cook
- ☑  probe him about the company, the way they like things done and how you might find the superintendents that you will come across
- ☑  any bridge and engine room equipment problems and any peculiarities
- ☑  any hull or structural damage and next scheduled dry-docking
- ☑  is ship fully stored?
- ☑  if you are unfamiliar with the port and the next scheduled port, ask about these and any problems with navigation, port facilities or officials
- ☑  if you can, check the bond, although it is probably sealed. At least see the final bond statement
- ☑  check the cash and make sure you have the safe keys and the combination
- ☑  communications with the company. Run through the email system or any other system being used.

Ship's certificates and status. Check these against the checklist and also verify:

☑ Validity
☑ expiry dates
☑ any renewals or extensions required to cover the forthcoming voyage
☑ that they are complete.

These include the ship's certificate of registration issued by the Flag State and the statutory certificates that may be issued by a Classification Society. If any of the certificates are ashore with the agent, make sure you have the receipt.

The Master should be fully familiar with:

☑ The company's documented SMS
☑ the lines of communication and responsibilities
☑ any peculiarities of the vessel's SMS
☑ the documented Ship Security Plan (SSP)
☑ the lines of communication under the SSP
☑ any other standing instructions prior to assuming full command.

Any non-conformity regarding an item of maintenance or concerning a section of the SMS should be reported and corrective action taken.

Charter and cargo. You should:

☑ Be made aware of the charterer and their contact details
☑ be made aware of the terms and conditions of the charter party
☑ seek input where required from the Chief Officer and Chief Engineer as to the performance ability of the vessel
☑ clarify with the company any item of the charter party that you have any doubts about or the vessel's ability to perform the charterer's requirements.

On a general inspection of the vessel, you should pay particular attention to the condition of:

- ☑ Anchors and their arrangements
- ☑ mooring arrangements/condition of the mooring lines
- ☑ watertight doors
- ☑ ventilation heads
- ☑ hatch covers including dogs and clamps
- ☑ hatch access covers including dogs and clamps
- ☑ scuppers and their plugs
- ☑ rubber gaskets.

Fire and safety equipment. Ensure that:

- ☑ Lifesaving equipment is in order
- ☑ fire protection, detection and extinguishing systems are available
- ☑ a copy of the fire control plan is stored in a prominent location
- ☑ fire equipment lockers, including breathing apparatus sets, are in order
- ☑ fire dampers operate
- ☑ any watertight doors and fire doors operate
- ☑ other fire-fighting equipment is operational and in order.

General. Before the commencement of the voyage, check:

- ☑ All medicines required to be in the medicine stores are actually onboard and are within their expiry dates, with any out-of-date medication replaced immediately
- ☑ check the charts and courses laid off.

You should satisfy yourself that the vessel is in a seaworthy condition and that the crew are qualified and certificated for the voyage and cover any requirements of the Flag State. If you find any shortcomings in this regard, which you believe could affect the safety and/or seaworthiness of the vessel, you must immediately report these to the company, even if the situation suggests there is insufficient time to rectify these deficiencies before commencing the voyage. There will be instances where the Class Society and/or Flag

State administration may require these deficiencies to be rectified before commencing the voyage.

The procedure of taking over command should be properly documented in the vessel's SMS records and acknowledged in writing by both the relieving and the relieved Master.

The outgoing Master should show you round the bridge and this is your opportunity to have not only the basic operation of unfamiliar bridge equipment explained to you, but also their idiosyncrasies.

Ask about the handling of the ship. What is the power of the thrusters if you have them? Right hand or left hand propellers? If variable pitch, which way does the bow sheer when going astern? If there are standard propellers and engines, how many movements can be made before the air bottles need topping up and how long before you can make the next movement? There are obviously many more questions so remember that, once the leaving Master is down the gangway, you are on your own. Don't forget your cabin keys!

# 19 Emergency Checklist

## 19.1 Collision

### Initial

- ☑ Manoeuvre own vessel to minimise the effects of collision
- ☑ sound general alarm/ship's whistle
- ☑ muster crew and passengers (with lifejackets)
- ☑ close all watertight doors and fire doors
- ☑ issue distress/urgency message to all stations.

### Actions on Impact

- ☑ Switch on deck lighting and exhibit NUC signals
- ☑ if vessels remain embedded together, agreement should be made to remain fixed in this position until action has been taken to restrict flooding. This may require one vessel maintaining ahead propulsion
- ☑ investigate damage and initiate control measures, including pollution:
  - determine the vessel's position and the available depth of water
  - sound tanks/ship spaces
- ☑ offer assistance to, or request assistance from, the other vessel involved if required
- ☑ consider the loss of stability, taking into account free surface effect of any flooded compartments
- ☑ consider salvage assistance
- ☑ consider beaching if own vessel is sinking
- ☑ establish communications with the other vessel and exchange the following information:
  - name
  - port of registry
  - port of departure
  - port of destination

- ☑ update Coastguard or RCC, keep crew informed
- ☑ inform company
- ☑ if own ship can safely move, proceed to the nearest safe refuge and moor your vessel securely. Your own vessel may currently be a danger to navigation
- ☑ log all events in the Bridge Movement Book
- ☑ record all details of the incident in the Deck Log Book, Official Log Book and on an incident report form.

## 19.1.1 After the event

- ☑ You should not discuss the collision with anyone unless the correspondent or lawyer appointed by the company, hull and machinery insurer or P&I insurer is present
  (If there is pollution caused by the escape of oil from the other vessel, the insurance cover provided by the hull and machinery insurer may be involved. In such cases, the hull and machinery insurer or their correspondents must be contacted)
- ☑ it is advisable to lodge a note of protest in some jurisdictions to protect the right to claim against the other vessel. You should seek advice from your P&I correspondent or lawyer
- ☑ after taking the necessary preventative measures, you should ensure all witnesses make a record of their recollection of events and the run up to the collision. You should counsel any witnesses to give an honest account of the incident as they saw it, even if they believe that this is to the detriment of the vessel. Any photographs or video footage captured by the crew should be gathered. A suitable incentive could be offered to any member of the crew who has collected such evidence
- ☑ any VHF correspondence between the vessels involved (or with the shore/port/VTS) in the run up to the collision should be recorded in writing to show what exchange of information/ warnings were conveyed
- ☑ if your ship has ECDIS, the data for this period should be stored as soon as possible.

You should liaise with your P&I correspondent/lawyer to confirm the other details they require, but copies of the following documents, together with the vessel's trading documents, will need to be retained:

- ☑ Chart used (paper or electronic) – do not tamper with or erase any marks/data
- ☑ Deck Log Book
- ☑ Bridge Movement Book
- ☑ any scrap logs
- ☑ Engine Log Book
- ☑ Engine Movement Book
- ☑ course recorder printouts
- ☑ records of working and rest hours of the Master, officers and crew on duty.

## 19.2 Grounding

- ☑ Stop engines
- ☑ sound general alarm/ship's whistle
- ☑ muster crew and passengers (with lifejackets)
- ☑ close all watertight doors and fire doors
- ☑ if assistance is required urgently, send a PAN-PAN message to all stations. Otherwise, inform the Coastguard by VHF
- ☑ exhibit signals for vessel aground:
  - day – three black balls
  - night – anchor lights plus two all round red lights
- ☑ commence appropriate sound signal if in restricted visibility
- ☑ update AIS status
- ☑ ensure 'high' sea suction in use
- ☑ investigate vessel damage, including pollution, and initiate control measures:
  - sound all tanks and ship spaces
  - sound all round vessel, consider using rescue boat if required
  - confirm vessel's position and depth of water, including direction of navigable water
- ☑ determine whether the wind or sea is carrying the vessel into further difficulties. If so, consider using the anchors
- ☑ keep all ship's departments, including passengers, informed
- ☑ inform the DPA/company, and keep updated.
- ☑ before taking further action, consider all relevant information including:
  - weather and sea state
  - state/height and range of tide
  - nature of seabed
  - depth of water all round the vessel
  - damaged stability condition
- ☑ in lightening the vessel, consider the discharge of the following and the resultant change of stability, draught, trim and list:
  - water ballast
  - fresh water
  - survival craft and passengers
  - stores

- ☑ consider contacting class or company, as appropriate, to determine stability in damaged condition
- ☑ if unable to float safely by the vessel's own efforts, call for assistance
- ☑ log all events in the Bridge Movement Book
- ☑ record all details of the incident in the Deck Log Book, Official Log Book and on incident report form.

## 19.2.1 Records after a grounding

Evidence to be gathered following a grounding:

- ☑ Date and exact time of the grounding
- ☑ position of the grounding
- ☑ detailed description of the section of the vessel aground
- ☑ nature of the seabed where the grounding has taken place
- ☑ courses at the time of the grounding (charted, steered, gyro and magnetic)
- ☑ speed at the time of the grounding (RPM or pitch setting)
- ☑ rudder angle at the time of the grounding
- ☑ alterations of course and/or speed in the period immediately before the grounding
- ☑ orders given
- ☑ communications exchanged between ship and shore
- ☑ if under pilotage, any communications with the pilot and or tugs prior to the grounding
- ☑ detail of positions plotted prior to the grounding
- ☑ helm/engine movements before/after the grounding
- ☑ weather conditions at the time of the grounding
- ☑ tide and current at the time of the grounding
- ☑ draught at the time of the grounding
- ☑ soundings around the vessel
- ☑ soundings of all the ship's tanks from the last record before grounding, and the situation after the grounding
- ☑ cargo distribution from the last record before grounding and the situation after the grounding.

Navigation and communication equipment in use at the time of the grounding:

- ☑ Echo sounder information/range used/printout
- ☑ radar/ARPA settings and any adjustments/changes to these settings and the time of such change prior to the incident
- ☑ GPS positions
- ☑ VHF – location of the radio in use and channels in operation/being monitored
- ☑ ECDIS – chart used and last update
- ☑ any other navigation/comms equipment in use.

## Persons involved

Record the name, rank, duties and location for:

- ☑ All persons on the bridge at the time of the grounding
- ☑ any further eye witnesses
- ☑ engine room personnel
- ☑ pilot's details
- ☑ other vessels/traffic in the area at the time of the grounding.

You should liaise with your P&I correspondent/lawyer to confirm whether they require any other details, but copies of the following documents, together with the vessel's trading documents, will need to be retained:

- ☑ Chart used (paper or electronic) – do not tamper with or erase any marks/data
- ☑ Deck Log Book
- ☑ Bridge Movement Book
- ☑ any scrap logs
- ☑ Engine Log Book
- ☑ Engine Movement Book
- ☑ course recorder printouts
- ☑ records of working and rest hours of the Master, officers and crew on duty.

## 19.3  Man Overboard

**Initial actions**

- ☑ Let go quick release buoy
- ☑ turn ship/hand steering/commence recovery manoeuvre
- ☑ initiate position fix on satnav/GPS/electronic chart
- ☑ sound alarm/3 long blasts
- ☑ maintain visual contact/post lookout
- ☑ Master to bridge.

**Subsequent actions**

- ☑ Engines on standby
- ☑ inform engine room
- ☑ distress/urgency broadcast
- ☑ muster crew/communications established
- ☑ prepare rescue boat/medical party stand by
- ☑ flag signal 'O'
- ☑ deck preparations for recovery:
    - • deck lights
    - • pilot ladder
    - • cargo net/equipment
    - • heaving line
    - • line throwing apparatus.

**Notes**

In turning the ship:

- ☑ If the MOB is visible, turn the ship in the direction of the MOB
- ☑ if in visual contact with the MOB, turn vessel to maintain contact
- ☑ do not initially stop the ship. Turning the ship will slow it down and speed can be reduced thereafter.

Where someone has fallen overboard or is found to be missing, the cover provided by the P&I Club is involved. You should contact your company and your P&I Club or their local correspondent.

## 19.4  Fire

### Initial

- ☑ Determine location of fire
- ☑ acknowledge the alarm
- ☑ send fire party, with radio(s), to investigate:
  - • location
  - • extent
  - • type of fire
- ☑ close down the vessel as quickly as possible (fans, vents, watertight doors).

### Actions

- ☑ Sound fire alarm
- ☑ start fire pumps
- ☑ exhibit NUC signals/shapes
- ☑ update AIS.

### Bridge

- ☑ Alter course and speed to minimise any effects of fire/smoke
- ☑ confirm vessel's position
- ☑ appraise yourself of the location of any hazards
- ☑ muster crew and passengers
- ☑ close fire doors
- ☑ instigate a search for any missing persons (if applicable).

### Actions

- ☑ Close down manual fire dampers and vent flaps
- ☑ isolate electrical supplies
- ☑ commence taking a log of events, including position
- ☑ make appropriate PA announcement to passengers/crew.

## Communications

- ☑ Inform the Coastguard (in port, call the fire brigade) and DPA/Duty Manager. You should advise them of the following information:
  - Position of vessel
  - nature and size of fire (details of cargo)
  - number of passengers and crew onboard
  - measures currently being taken to fight or contain the fire
  - nature of assistance required.

## Actions

- ☑ Initiate fire containment and fire-fighting measures
- ☑ consider effects on stability including free surface.

## If fire is getting worse or is out of control:

- ☑ Consider using fixed fire-fighting system
- ☑ consider anchoring vessel
- ☑ update Fire Brigade/Coastguard
- ☑ consider abandoning ship.

## If fire is extinguished or well under control:

- ☑ Consider temperature/likelihood of re-ignition
- ☑ check adjacent compartments to ensure fire has not spread through heat transfer
- ☑ consider restoring ventilation to clear smoke
- ☑ update Fire Brigade/Coastguard
- ☑ record details of incident in Deck Log Book, Official Log Book and on incident report form.

## 19.5 Dangerous Goods Incident

- ☑ Sound general alarm/ship's whistle
- ☑ muster crew in a safe area upwind of the hazard
- ☑ close watertight and automatic fire doors
- ☑ shut down fans and mechanical ventilation
- ☑ start fire pumps
- ☑ put additional electrical generators in ready state
- ☑ confirm vessel's position and proximity of hazards
- ☑ issue distress or urgency signal (as appropriate) to all stations
- ☑ exhibit NUC signal
- ☑ determine which dangerous good(s) are involved
- ☑ consult EMS Guide (Emergency Procedures) within IMDG supplement to determine:
  - actions in event of spillage
  - actions in event of fire
  - first aid equipment ready, consult MFAG (Medical First Aid Guide)
- ☑ assess risks and whether it is safe for crew to enter the affected area to investigate cause/extent of incident, using the appropriate PPE
- ☑ fight fire and control/remove any spillage in accordance with EMS guidelines
- ☑ if crew can be sent safely to the affected area:
  - close all watertight/weathertight openings
  - secure the cargo using all available means
  - determine any leakage of fuel or dangerous goods
- ☑ consider jettisoning of cargo
- ☑ can the voyage be safely resumed? If not, determine the nearest safe port or anchorage
- ☑ keep ship's departments and passengers updated
- ☑ notify the company/DPA
- ☑ update Coastguard or RCC
- ☑ record details of the incident in Deck Log Book, Official Log Book and on incident report form.

## 19.6 Cargo Shift

- ☑ Sound general alarm/ship's whistle
- ☑ muster crew and passengers (with lifejackets) preferably on the high side of the vessel if listed
- ☑ close watertight doors
- ☑ exhibit NUC signal
- ☑ confirm vessel's position and proximity of hazards
- ☑ reduce speed and manoeuvre the vessel to minimise motion
- ☑ if there is danger of capsizing or flooding, issue distress or urgency signal (as appropriate) to all stations and prepare for abandonment
- ☑ assess risks and investigate cause/extent of shift
- ☑ assess stability and confirm angle of loll
- ☑ if crew can be safely sent to the affected area:
  - • close all watertight/weathertight openings
  - • secure the cargo using all available means
  - • determine any leakage of fuel or dangerous goods
- ☑ is it safe and prudent to use water ballast to correct list or trim?
- ☑ consider jettisoning of cargo
- ☑ can the voyage be safely resumed? If not, determine the nearest safe port or anchorage
- ☑ keep personnel updated
- ☑ notify the company/DPA
- ☑ update Coastguard or RCC
- ☑ record details of the incident in Deck Log Book and Official Log Book.

## 19.7  Salvage/Search and Rescue (SAR)

- ☑ Establish communication with the casualty and the Coastguard
- ☑ implement rescue boat drill to gather resources and crew to prepare for the situation
- ☑ advise the passengers of the situation. Consider seeking any medical practitioners onboard if necessary
- ☑ advise the following of the ship's ETA at the casualty:
    - Coastguard station coordinating the search and rescue
    - coordinator of the surface search (CSS) – if applicable
    - on scene commander (OSC) – if applicable
- ☑ where practical, use radar to identify and plot the casualty and other ships proceeding to the scene
- ☑ keep a full log of events and a full log of communications
- ☑ increase the bridge team as required (post extra lookouts)
- ☑ advise the CSS, OSC or casualty of the following resources that the ship has available:
    - lifesaving equipment
    - medical equipment
    - fire-fighting equipment
    - fast rescue boat
    - reception and catering facilities
- ☑ while proceeding to the scene, order adequate preparation to be made for recovery and reception of survivors, including preparation for helicopter operations
- ☑ once on the scene, if the casualty has not been located, initiate the surface search (refer to the IAMSAR Manual)
- ☑ when the casualty is located, follow the directions of the CSS. If there is no CSS, consider the most appropriate action to recover survivors (refer to the IAMSAR Manual)
- ☑ agree rescue boat operating and communication procedure with the bridge
- ☑ rig guest warp, over side ladders and additional painters
- ☑ rig additional over side lighting for the rescue boat
- ☑ inform the Duty Manager
- ☑ record details of incident in Deck Log Book, Official Log Book and on incident report form.

### 19.7.1 Records when salvor is in attendance

Salvage costs concern the hull and machinery and cargo insurers. You should therefore immediately contact your company and the hull and machinery insurer, enabling them to decide what actions to take.

Whenever a salvor is in attendance, you should keep a detailed chronological record of the following items:

- ☑ Weather, wind, sea and tidal conditions from commencement of the refloating operation
- ☑ names and position of tugs in attendance
- ☑ times that tugs commenced the refloating operation
- ☑ each activity undertaken and the result achieved
- ☑ materials used by the salvor
- ☑ personnel involved
- ☑ any damage to the salvor's equipment
- ☑ communication with the salvors.

During a refloating operation, you should keep a detailed record of the vessel's expenses and excess costs incurred in respect of:

- ☑ Crew involvement (name, time and activity involved)
- ☑ fuel used (heavy fuel, diesel and lubrication oil)
- ☑ vessel's equipment used and damaged.

## 19.8  Medical

- ☑ Administer first aid:
    - ensure own safety
    - get assistance – if possible, establish whether there are any medical practitioners onboard
    - administer immediate treatment – airway, breathing and circulation
    - check whether casualty is conscious/unconscious
    - assess blood loss/clinical shock
- ☑ provide medical care and make the patient as comfortable as possible.

### Signs and Symptoms

- ☑ Signs and symptoms to check include:
    - respiration/breathing
    - pulse rate
    - blood pressure
    - temperature
    - injuries/bruising/wounds/bleeding
    - faeces/urine/sputum/vomit
- ☑ consult the 'Ship Master's Medical Guide'
- ☑ obtain as much of the following information/history as possible:
    - name and nationality
    - age and sex
    - address
    - medical history
    - medication taken/required
    - what countries the patient has recently visited
- ☑ establish the ship's position/ETA of nearest port
- ☑ if in mid-ocean, consult ALRS for radio advice, eg CIRM Rome
- ☑ if sufficiently close to port, arrange ambulance/medical services for arrival

- ☑ if coastal, call Coastguard/RCC using urgency message requesting medical assistance
- ☑ where 'Medivac' is requested, prepare for helicopter or ship to ship transfer
- ☑ inform the DPA/Duty Manager
- ☑ record details of incident in Deck Log Book, Official Log Book, Medical Log Book and on an incident report form.

## 19.9  Helicopter Operations

See Section 4.7 for specific helicopter actions.

- ☑ Contact Coastguard/Pilot Station and securite/urgency broadcast as required
- ☑ advise all ship's departments
- ☑ determine rendezvous time and position
- ☑ paperwork prepared:
    - relevant emergency information, fire plans, crew list, etc or
    - casualty evacuation checklist, medical history and personal documentation.

# 19.10 Pollution Incident (Oil Tanker)

Immediate action

- ☑ Sound emergency alarm

Initial response

- ☑ Stop all cargo and/or bunkering operations
- ☑ close manifold valves
- ☑ switch air conditioning to recirculation or stop air intake to accommodation
- ☑ stop non-essential air intake fans to the engine room
- ☑ locate source of leakage and stop/reduce oil
- ☑ consult SOPEP plan
- ☑ consult MSDS/EMS guideline
- ☑ assess fire risk from release of flammable substances
- ☑ start fire pump
- ☑ commence clean-up procedures using absorbents and permitted solvents
- ☑ advise relevant parties (local authorities, coastal State, DPA/ company, P&I correspondent, etc).

Secondary response

- ☑ Reduce the oil level in the tank concerned by transferring oil into an empty or slack tank
- ☑ reduce level of oil in tanks in the suspected area
- ☑ drain affected line to empty or slack tank
- ☑ reduce inert gas pressure to zero
- ☑ if the leakage is at the pumproom sea valve, relieve pressure on pipelines
- ☑ prepare pumps for transfer of oil to other tanks or to shore or lightering vessel
- ☑ prepare portable pumps if it is possible to transfer spilt oil to empty tank

- ☑ consider pumping water into the leaking tank to create water cushion and prevent further oil loss. If leakage is below the waterline, arrange divers for further investigation
- ☑ calculate stresses/stability. If necessary, request shore assistance
- ☑ transfer cargo or bunkers to alleviate high stability stresses
- ☑ carefully stow residue from the clean-up operation prior to disposal.

## 19.11 Abandon Ship

- ☑ Issue distress/mayday
- ☑ sound general emergency alarm
- ☑ close watertight and remote fire doors
- ☑ have crew prepare for abandonment
  - muster check all crew and passengers, who should be wearing warm clothing, lifejackets or survival suits where appropriate
  - bring additional equipment to the embarkation deck, eg blankets, first aid kit, torches, distress flares, etc
- ☑ lower lifeboats to embarkation deck and rig painters
- ☑ activate EPIRB and SART and bring to the lifeboats
- ☑ take VDR (Voyage Data Recorder) cassette if possible
- ☑ can the vessel be re-boarded (if necessary)?
- ☑ update mayday
- ☑ when ready, give the order to abandon ship.

Once clear of vessel:

- ☑ Ensure that all crew are accounted for in survival craft
- ☑ ensure that all survival craft are secured together and restrained from drifting away from the vessel separately
- ☑ issue seasickness tablets.

## 19.12 Angle of Loll

Angle of loll is caused by a rise in the height of the centre of gravity (KG) so that it creates a negative metacentric height (GM). There are several reasons why this can develop on a voyage, including:

- Burning of fuel or water lowering G and introducing free surface effect (FSE)
- water absorption in hygroscopic cargoes, eg timber deck cargoes
- water trapped on deck, eg within pipes on offshore vessels
- ice accretion on deck
- cargo shift
- flooding.

Angle of Loll should be rectified by reducing the height of the centre of gravity. Care must be taken not to cause the vessel to list quickly in the opposite direction as this could be sufficient to take the vessel beyond the angle of vanishing stability and capsize it.

- ☑ Alter course putting the ship into the waves, keeping the high side into the wind
- ☑ confirm the listed condition is due to the angle of loll:
  - check port and starboard listing moments are equal
  - check for slack tanks
- ☑ press up any slack tanks, one at a time and the smallest first to remove FSE
- ☑ discharge any high ballast wing tank
- ☑ where 3 double bottom tanks are available, load ballast into the middle tank first
- ☑ when only 2 double bottom ballast tanks are available, load into the lowest (listed side) double bottom tanks
- ☑ if necessary, jettisoning deck cargo can be considered.

It is important that only one tank at a time is worked, and it should be remembered that when loading into low sided tanks or discharging into high sided tanks the vessel may initially list further. The situation should improve as the height of the centre of gravity reduces.

INDEX